FINISH LINE

Mathematics
for the Common Core State Standards

Continental

ISBN 978-0-8454-6763-3

Table of Contents

Welcome to Finish Line Mathematics for the Common Core State Standards

About This Book

Finish Line Mathematics for the Common Core State Standards will help you prepare for math tests. Each year in math class, you learn new skills and ideas. This book focuses on the math skills and ideas that are the most important for each grade. It is important to master the concepts you learn each year because mathematical ideas and skills build on each other. The things you learn this year will help you understand and master the skills you will learn next year.

This book has units of related lessons. Each lesson concentrates on one main math idea. The lesson reviews things you have learned in math class. It provides explanations and examples. Along the side of each lesson page are reminders to help you recall what you learned in earlier grades.

After the lesson come three pages of practice problems. The problems are the same kinds you find on most math tests. The first page has multiple-choice, or selected-response, problems. Each item has four answers to choose from, and you must select the best answer. At the top of the page is a sample problem with a box beneath it that explains how to find the answer. Then there are a number of problems for you to do on your own.

Constructed-response, or short-answer, items are on the next page. You must answer these items using your own words. Usually, you will need to show your work or write an explanation of your answer in these items. This type of problem helps you demonstrate that you know how to do operations and carry out procedures. They also show that you understand the skill. Again, the first item is a sample and its answer is explained. You will complete the rest of the items by yourself.

The last page has one or two extended-response problems. These items are like the short writing items, but they have more parts and are often a little harder. The first part may ask you to solve a problem and show your work. The second may ask you to explain how you found your answer or why it is correct. This item has a hint to point you in the right direction.

At the end of each unit is a review section. The problems in it cover all the different skills and ideas in the lessons of that unit. The review contains multiple-choice, constructed-response, and extended-response items.

A practice test and a glossary appear at the end of the book. The practice test gives you a chance to try out what you've learned. You will need to use all the skills you have reviewed and practiced in the book on the practice test. The glossary lists important words and terms along with their definitions to help you remember them.

The Goals of Learning Math

Math is everywhere in the world around you. You use math more than you probably realize to help you understand and make sense of that world. But what does it mean to be good at math?

To be good at math, you need to practice certain habits. And you need the right attitude.

- You make sense of problems and do not give up in solving them. You make sure you understand the problem before you try to solve it. You form a plan and then carry out that plan to find an answer. Along the way, you ask yourself if what you are doing makes sense. And if you do not figure out the answer on the first try, you try another way.

- You think about numbers using symbols. You can think about a real-life situation as numbers and operations.

- You draw conclusions about situations and support them with proof. You use what you know about numbers and operations to provide reasons for your conclusions and predictions. When you read or hear someone else's explanation, you think about it and decide if it makes sense. You ask questions that help you better understand the ideas.

- You model with mathematics. You represent real-life problems with a drawing or diagram, a graph, or an equation. You decide if your model makes sense.

- You use the right tools at the right time. You know how to use rulers, protractors, calculators, and other tools. More importantly, you know when to use them.

- You are careful and accurate in your work. You calculate correctly and label answers. You use the correct symbols and definitions. You choose exactly the right words for your explanations and descriptions.

- You look for structure in math. You see how different parts of math are related or connected. You can use an idea you already know to help you understand a new idea. You make connections between things you have already learned and new ideas.

- You look for the patterns in math. When you see the patterns, you can find shortcuts to use that still lead you to the correct answer. You are able to decide if your shortcut worked or not.

These habits help you master new mathematical ideas so that you can remember and use them. All of these habits will make math easier to understand and to do. And that will make it a great tool to use in your everyday life!

Ratio, Proportion, and Percent

- **Lesson 1 Rates** reviews rates and unit rates involving fractions and how to use them to solve problems.

- **Lesson 2 Solving Proportions** reviews what proportions are and how to use them to solve problems.

- **Lesson 3 Proportional Relationships** reviews how to apply proportions in situations using equations and tables.

- **Lesson 4 Graphing Proportional Relationships** reviews how to graph and interpret the graph of a proportional situation.

- **Lesson 5 Solving Percent Problems** reviews how to use proportions to solve problems involving percents.

- **Lesson 6 More Percent Problems** reviews how to solve percent problems that have more than one step.

Rates

7.RP.1

Some examples of rates with different units of measure are

dollars per ounce
miles per hour
bags per square feet

A **complex fraction** is a fraction that has a fraction in the numerator, the denominator, or both.

Dividing fractions is the same as multiplying by the reciprocal of the second number.

$$\frac{3}{8} \div \frac{2}{5} = \frac{3}{8} \times \frac{5}{2}$$

To multiply a fraction by a whole number, rewrite the whole number as a fraction divided by 1.

$$8 \times \frac{5}{6} = \frac{8}{1} \times \frac{5}{6}$$

A **rate** compares two quantities with different units. A rate that compares a quantity to one unit of another quantity is called a **unit rate.** A unit rate is a rate with a denominator of 1.

Grady types $\frac{2}{3}$ of a page in $\frac{1}{3}$ hour. What is the unit rate?

The rate is pages per hour.

Write the rate as a complex fraction: $\dfrac{\frac{2}{3}}{\frac{1}{3}}$

Divide the numerator by the denominator.

$$\frac{\frac{2}{3}}{\frac{1}{3}} = \frac{2}{3} \div \frac{1}{3} = \frac{2}{3} \times \frac{3}{1} = \frac{6}{3} = \frac{2}{1}$$

The unit rate is $\frac{2}{1}$, or 2 pages per hour.

Unit rates can be used to solve problems.

Every $\frac{3}{4}$-cup serving of custard uses $\frac{1}{2}$ cup of milk. How many cups of milk are in 6 servings?

Find the unit rate, or cups of milk per one serving.

$$\frac{\frac{1}{2}}{\frac{3}{4}} = \frac{1}{2} \div \frac{3}{4} = \frac{1}{2} \times \frac{4}{3} = \frac{4}{6} = \frac{2}{3} \text{ cup per 1 serving}$$

Multiply the unit rate by 6.

$$\frac{2}{3} \times 6 = \frac{2}{3} \times \frac{6}{1} = \frac{12}{3} = 4$$

There are 4 cups of milk in 6 servings.

SAMPLE Jeff paddles a canoe $\frac{3}{5}$ mile in $\frac{1}{4}$ hour. At this rate, how far does Jeff paddle in $1\frac{1}{2}$ hours?

A $\frac{9}{40}$ mile B $1\frac{13}{20}$ miles C $2\frac{2}{5}$ miles D $3\frac{3}{5}$ miles

The correct answer is D. First find the unit rate, to show how many miles Jeff paddles in one hour. The unit rate is $\frac{\frac{3}{5}}{\frac{1}{4}} = \frac{3}{5} \div \frac{1}{4} = \frac{3}{5} \times \frac{4}{1} = \frac{12}{5} = 2\frac{2}{5}$ miles in one hour. Then multiply the unit rate by the total time: $2\frac{2}{5} \times 1\frac{1}{2} = \frac{12}{5} \times \frac{3}{2} = \frac{36}{10} = 3\frac{6}{10} = 3\frac{3}{5}$. Jeff paddles $3\frac{3}{5}$ miles in $1\frac{1}{2}$ hours.

1 Gwen mows $\frac{1}{4}$ acre in $\frac{3}{4}$ hour. What fraction is used to find the unit rate, in acres per hour?

A $\frac{3}{4}$

C $\frac{4}{3}$

B $\frac{\frac{1}{4}}{\frac{3}{4}}$

D $\frac{\frac{3}{4}}{\frac{1}{4}}$

2 Don ate $\frac{1}{2}$ cup of vegetables. This was $\frac{2}{3}$ of a serving. What rate describes this?

A $\dfrac{\text{cups}}{\text{servings}} = \dfrac{\frac{1}{2}}{\frac{2}{3}}$

C $\dfrac{\text{servings}}{\text{cups}} = \dfrac{\frac{1}{2}}{\frac{2}{3}}$

B $\dfrac{\text{cups}}{\text{servings}} = \dfrac{\frac{2}{3}}{\frac{1}{2}}$

D $\dfrac{\text{servings}}{\text{cups}} = \dfrac{\frac{2}{3}}{\frac{1}{2}}$

3 Cathy's heart beats 12 times in $\frac{1}{6}$ minute. How many times does her heart beat in 60 minutes?

A 120

C 3,000

B 720

D 4,320

4 A jet flies 600 kilometers in $\frac{3}{4}$ hour. How far can this jet fly in $\frac{1}{2}$ hour?

A 225 km

C 480 km

B 400 km

D 1,600 km

5 A lawn with an area of 300 square feet needs $\frac{1}{2}$ pound of grass seed. How many pounds of grass seed are needed for a lawn that is 60 feet long and 20 feet wide?

A 2

C 6

B 4

D 8

SAMPLE Amy bought $\frac{7}{8}$ pound of rice for $0.70. At this rate, how many pounds of rice can she buy for $5?

Answer _____

First find the unit rate for the rice, in dollars per pound: $\frac{0.70}{\frac{7}{8}} =$ $0.70 \div \frac{7}{8} = 0.70 \times \frac{8}{7} = \frac{5.6}{7} = 0.80$ or $0.80 per pound. To find the number of pounds Amy can buy for $5, divide $5 by the unit rate: $5 \div $0.80 = 6.25. So, she can buy 6.25 pounds of rice for $5.

6 A machine can scan 12 pages in $\frac{3}{5}$ minute. How many pages can be scanned in 1 minute?

Answer _____

7 A $\frac{3}{8}$-pound piece of cheese contains 4 servings. How much cheese is in 1 serving?

Answer _____

8 Damien paints $\frac{1}{5}$ of a room in $\frac{5}{12}$ hour. What unit rate describes this situation?

Answer _____

9 Wilfredo buys $\frac{2}{5}$ pound of mixed nuts for $2.50. At this rate, how many pounds of mixed nuts can he buy for $10?

Answer _____

10 A tree grows $\frac{1}{4}$ foot in $\frac{1}{12}$ year.

Part A Write the rate at which this tree grows as a fraction.

Answer _____

Part B How many feet does the tree grow in 1 year? Explain how you know.

_____

_____

_____

11 In $\frac{1}{6}$ hour, José jogged $\frac{7}{10}$ mile.

Part A Write a fraction that can be used to find the unit rate for this situation.

Answer _____

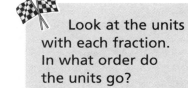

Look at the units with each fraction. In what order do the units go?

Part B At this rate, how many miles can José jog in $\frac{1}{2}$ hour? Explain how you know.

_____

_____

_____

_____

LESSON

2

Solving Proportions

7.RP.2.a–c, 7.RP.3

A **cross product** is the product of the denominator of one fraction and the numerator of the other. If the cross products of two ratios are equal, they form a proportion.

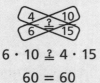

$$6 \cdot 10 \stackrel{?}{=} 4 \cdot 15$$

$$60 = 60$$

To simplify ratios, divide the numerator and the denominator by their greatest common factor.

Variables, or letters such as n or x, are often used to represent unknown quantities in proportions.

A **proportion** shows that two ratios are equal. To see if two ratios form a proportion, simplify each ratio to see if they are equal.

Train A was on time $\frac{16}{20}$ of the time. Train B was on time $\frac{24}{30}$ of the time. Are these ratios proportional?

Simplify $\frac{16}{20}$: $\frac{16 \div 4}{20 \div 4} = \frac{4}{5}$

Simplify $\frac{24}{30}$: $\frac{24 \div 6}{30 \div 6} = \frac{4}{5}$

Both ratios simplify to $\frac{4}{5}$, so yes, they are proportional.

Proportions can be used to solve problems.

The ratios of times that trains C and D were on time are proportional. Train C was on time 15 out of 20 times this month. Train D ran 36 times this month. How many of these times was train D on time?

Write a proportion to show the two ratios are equal. Let x represent the unknown quantity.

$$\frac{15}{20} = \frac{x}{36}$$

Write the cross products.

$$20 \cdot x = 15 \cdot 36$$

Simplify and solve for x.

$$20x = 540$$
$$x = 540 \div 20 = 27$$

Train D was on time 27 times.

UNIT 1
Ratio, Proportion, and Percent

12

© The Continental Press, Inc.   DUPLICATING THIS MATERIAL IS ILLEGAL.

SAMPLE The lengths and widths of two rectangles are proportional. One rectangle is 6 inches by 8 inches. What could be the dimensions of the other rectangle?

    A 4 inches by 6 inches   **C** 9 inches by 12 inches

    B 6 inches by 9 inches   **D** 12 inches by 18 inches

The correct answer is C. The dimensions of the given rectangle form the ratio $\frac{6}{8}$, which simplifies to $\frac{3}{4}$. Write and simplify a ratio for each answer choice to see which equals this. Choice A = $\frac{4}{6}$ = $\frac{2}{3}$. Choice B = $\frac{6}{9}$ = $\frac{2}{3}$. Choice C = $\frac{9}{12}$ = $\frac{3}{4}$. Choice D = $\frac{12}{18}$ = $\frac{2}{3}$. Only choice C simplifies to $\frac{3}{4}$.

1 To make a certain shade of purple paint, different parts of red paint are mixed with different parts of blue paint. The table below shows this relationship.

Parts Red	6	8	12	16
Parts Blue	15	20	30	40

What is the ratio of parts red to parts blue?

A 2 parts red to 3 parts blue

B 2 parts red to 5 parts blue

C 3 parts red to 5 parts blue

D 3 parts red to 10 parts blue

2 Randall wrote the proportion below to find *n*, the cost of 3 pounds of fruit.

$$\frac{6}{5} = \frac{n}{3}$$

Which equation can be used to find *n*?

A $n = \frac{6}{5 \cdot 3}$ **C** $n = \frac{5}{6 \cdot 3}$

B $n = \frac{5 \cdot 3}{6}$ **D** $n = \frac{6 \cdot 3}{5}$

3 Which of the following ratios forms a proportion with $\frac{12}{16}$?

A $\frac{8}{12}$ **C** $\frac{18}{24}$

B $\frac{16}{20}$ **D** $\frac{24}{30}$

4 An elevator travels directly up 27 floors in 90 seconds. How many floors can this elevator travel directly up in 60 seconds?

A 18   **C** 40

B 21   **D** 200

5 This table shows the relationship between the cups of flour used to make muffins.

Cups of Flour	2	3	4
Number of Muffins	12	18	24

How many muffins can be made with 7 cups of flour?

A 13   **C** 36

B 30   **D** 42

SAMPLE A car travels 270 miles on 15 gallons of gas. How many gallons of gas are needed for this car to travel 100 miles?

Answer _____

Set up a proportion that compares miles traveled to gallons of gas used. Let x represent the unknown number of gallons: $\frac{270}{15} = \frac{100}{x}$. Cross multiply and then solve for x: $270 \cdot x = 15 \cdot 100$, $270x = 1{,}500$, $x = 1{,}500 \div 270 = 5\frac{5}{9}$ gallons.

6 Which of the following ratios are proportional?

$$\frac{9}{12} \qquad \frac{12}{15} \qquad \frac{16}{20} \qquad \frac{20}{24} \qquad \frac{24}{35}$$

Answer _____

7 This table shows proportional relationships.

12	20	24	48
3	5	6	12

What is the ratio that is common throughout this table, written in simplest form?

Answer _____

8 Clearance items in a store are all marked down proportionally. A shirt with an original price of $32 is on clearance for $12. What is the clearance price of a shirt with an original price of $40? Show your work.

Answer _____

9 A recipe calls for 3 parts water to 2 parts oats. Misty mixes $\frac{3}{4}$ cup of water with $\frac{1}{2}$ cup of oats.

> Write a ratio for each pair of numbers. Are the ratios equal?

Part A Is Misty following this recipe?

Answer _____

Part B Explain how you know your answer is correct.

_____

_____

_____

10 A video store charges the same fee each day a video is returned late. Craig returned a video 4 days late and paid a $3 fee.

Part A Write a proportional equation that can be used to find the late fee for a video that is returned 7 days late.

Answer _____

Part B What is the fee for a video that is returned 7 days late? Explain how you know.

_____

_____

_____

Proportional Relationships

7.RP.2.a–c

For a relationship to be proportional, *all* ratios of the relationship must be equivalent.

In the equation $y = ax$, the constant $a = \frac{y}{x}$.

The unit rate is a constant because it is always the same, no matter what the values of x and y are.

The equation $y = ax$ means "y is proportional to x for some constant a."

A **proportional relationship** can be represented in a table.

This table compares the sizes of different bottles of shampoo and the costs of the shampoo bottles.

Size (ounces)	12	24	42
Cost ($)	2	4	7

Are the prices of these shampoo bottles proportional?

Proportional quantities have equivalent ratios. Compare each ratio to see if they are all equivalent.

$$\frac{12 \text{ ounces}}{\$2} = \frac{6}{1} \qquad \frac{24 \text{ ounces}}{\$4} = \frac{6}{1} \qquad \frac{42 \text{ ounces}}{\$7} = \frac{6}{1}$$

All three ratios have a rate equal to $\frac{6}{1}$. So, the prices of the shampoo bottles are proportional.

Equations in the form $y = ax$ can also be used to represent proportional relationships. The variables x and y represent the values of each ratio in the proportion. The variable a represents the **constant,** or unit rate, for each ratio.

The cost of shampoo is proportional to the number of ounces in the bottle. Use the table above to write an equation to represent this relationship.

Since the cost of shampoo is proportional to the number of ounces, y represents the cost and x represents the number of ounces.

The constant $a = \frac{y}{x} = \frac{2}{12} = \frac{4}{24} = \frac{7}{42} = \frac{1}{6}$.

So, the equation for this proportional relationship is $y = \frac{1}{6}x$.

UNIT 1
Ratio, Proportion, and Percent

SAMPLE The cost of concert tickets is proportional to the number of tickets bought. Taylor bought 5 tickets and paid a total of $200. Which equation can be used to find the total cost for any number of concert tickets bought?

A $y = \frac{1}{40}x$ **B** $y = 40x$ **C** $y = \frac{1}{1,000}x$ **D** $y = 1,000x$

The correct answer is B. Since the total cost is proportional to the number of tickets, y represents the total cost and x represents the number of tickets. The constant a equals $\frac{y}{x} = \frac{\$200}{5 \text{ tickets}} = \frac{40}{1} = 40$. So, the equation to represent this proportional relationship is $y = 40x$.

1 Which of the following tables represents a proportional relationship?

A
2	4	6
1	2	4

C
2	4	6
4	5	6

B
2	4	6
3	5	7

D
2	4	6
5	10	15

2 The cooking time for a piece of meat is proportional to the weight of the meat. The table below shows this relationship.

Weight (lb)	1.5	2.5	3.5
Cooking Time (min)	30	50	70

What is the value of the constant for this proportional relationship?

A 20   **C** $\frac{1}{20}$

B 25   **D** $\frac{1}{25}$

3 The distance Trevor walks on a treadmill is proportional to the amount of time he walks. In $\frac{1}{4}$ hour, he walks $\frac{3}{4}$ mile. Which expression represents the value of the constant in this proportional relationship?

A $\frac{1}{4} + \frac{3}{4}$ **C** $\frac{3}{4} \cdot \frac{1}{4}$

B $\frac{1}{4} \div \frac{3}{4}$ **D** $\frac{3}{4} \div \frac{1}{4}$

4 Claudia earns the same dollar amount each hour she works. Last weekend, she worked a total of 9 hours and earned $72. Which equation can be used to find the total amount Claudia earns, y, for any number of hours, x, she works?

A $x = 8y$ **C** $x = 9y$

B $y = 8x$ **D** $y = 9x$

SAMPLE A 4-pound bag of oranges costs $5.00. A 10-pound bag of oranges costs $8.00. Is the cost per pound for these oranges proportional? Explain how you know.

Answer _____

Write ratios to compare the cost, in dollars, and pounds of each bag: $\frac{dollars}{pounds} = \frac{5}{4}$ and $\frac{dollars}{pounds} = \frac{8}{10} = 0.80$. These two ratios are not equal, so their cost per pound is not proportional.

5 The total cost to develop camera pictures is proportional to the number of pictures being developed. Margaret paid $5.50 to get 50 pictures developed. What number represents the constant in this proportional relationship?

Answer _____

6 Which quantities, if any, in this table are proportional?

A	B
10	5
12	6
16	8
20	10
32	16

Answer _____

7 The actual distance between cities is proportional to their measured distance on a map. The measured distance between two cities 75 miles apart is 3 inches on a map. Write an equation in the form $y = ax$ that can be used to find the actual distance between any two cities measured on a map.

Answer _____

UNIT 1 ▓▓▓▓▓▓▓▓▓▓▓▓▓▓▓▓▓▓▓▓▓▓▓▓▓▓▓▓▓▓▓▓▓▓▓▓
Ratio, Proportion, and Percent

8 The table below shows the relationship between the amount of paint used and the area of wall covered by the paint.

PAINT COVERAGE

Amount of Paint (quarts)	Area Covered (square feet)
$\frac{1}{2}$	40
$1\frac{1}{2}$	120
4	320
6	480

Part A Explain how you know this relationship is proportional.

_____

_____

_____

Part B Write an equation to represent this proportional relationship. Explain how you found this equation.

_____

_____

_____

_____

_____

What part of the relationship is represented by *x* and what part is represented by *y*?

Graphing Proportional Relationships

7.RP.2.a, b, d

Proportional relationships represented as equations are in the form $y = ax$.

To make a table of values, choose some values for x. Then substitute them into the equation to find the corresponding values of y.

Since weight cannot be negative, no negative integers are used on this graph.

To graph a point, start at the **origin, (0, 0).** Move left or right the number of units given by the x-coordinate. From there, move up or down the number of units given for the y-coordinate.

The graph of every proportional relationship will include the origin, the point (0, 0).

A proportional relationship represented as an equation can also be modeled on a **coordinate plane.**

At a salad bar, the price of salad, y, is proportional to the number of pounds of salad bought, x. The equation $y = 4x$ models this relationship. Draw a graph to model this relationship.

First make an x-y table of values for the equation.

x	y
1	4
2	8
3	12
4	16

On a blank coordinate plane, plot the points from the table you made and connect them with a straight line.

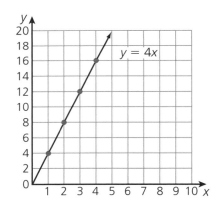

You can interpret a proportional relationship from its graph.

The point (2, 8) on the graph above shows that a salad weighing 2 pounds costs $8. What is the price per pound for the salad?

For each point on this graph, the x-coordinate represents the weight in pounds. The y-coordinate represents the cost. To find the price per pound, identify the point with an x-coordinate of 1. This is (1, 4). This means 1 pound of salad costs $4. So the price per pound is $4.

SAMPLE This graph shows the proportional relationship between the time a train travels and the distance it travels.

Which statement must be true?

A   In 1 hour, the train travels 50 miles.

B   In 1 hour, the train travels 100 miles.

C   In 5 hours, the train travels 200 miles.

D   In 5 hours, the train travels 500 miles.

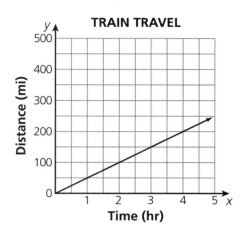

TRAIN TRAVEL

The correct answer is A. Since times of 1 hour and 5 hours are mentioned in the choices, identify the points with 1 and 5 as *x*-coordinates: (1, 50) and (5, 250). This means that in 1 hour the train travels 50 miles and in 5 hours, the train travels 250 miles.

1 Which point is located on the graph of any proportional relationship?

A   (0, 0)   C   (0, 1)

B   (1, 0)   D   (1, 1)

2 Which of the following graphs represents a proportional relationship?

A 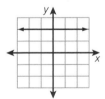   C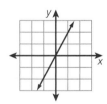

B 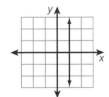   D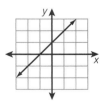

3 This graph shows the proportional relationship between the area of a floor, in square feet, and the total cost to carpet the floor.

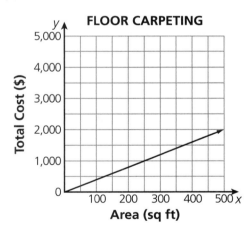

FLOOR CARPETING

What is the constant of proportionality?

A $1 per sq ft   C $5 per sq ft

B $4 per sq ft   D $10 per sq ft

SAMPLE The unit rate for a proportional relationship is $6. What two points must be located on the graph of the equation that models this relationship?

Answer _____

One point must be (0, 0) since the graph of every proportional relationship contains the origin. The given unit rate means that for 1 unit, the amount is $6. This is represented by the point (1, 6).

4 This graph shows the proportional relationship between lengths of each side of a regular polygon and the perimeter of the polygon.

What type of polygon is represented? Explain how you know.

_____

_____

_____

_____

_____

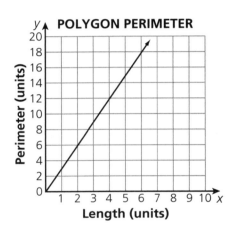

5 This graph shows the proportional relationship between the length of time a power tool is rented and the total cost to rent the power tool.

What is the constant of proportionality for this graph?

Answer _____

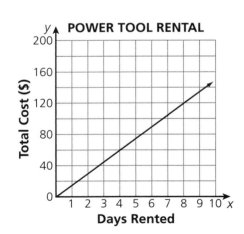

6 The number of calories in yogurt is proportional to the number of ounces of yogurt. A 6-ounce container of yogurt contains 120 calories.

Part A Draw the graph of this proportional relationship on the coordinate plane. Be sure to label each axis appropriately.

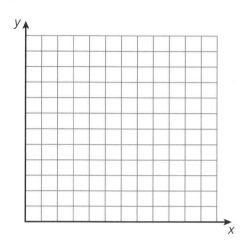

Part B How many calories are in a 4-ounce container of this yogurt? Explain how you know.

_____

_____

_____

How can you use the graph of this relationship to find the answer?

Solving Percent Problems

7.RP.3

Percent means "per 100." You can write n% as the ratio $\frac{n}{100}$.

A **proportion** shows that two ratios are equal.

$$\frac{15}{20} = \frac{75}{100}$$

A percent ratio has 100 in the denominator.

To change a percent to a fraction, write the percent in the numerator of a fraction with 100 in the denominator.

$$80\% = \frac{80}{100}$$

Proportions can be used to solve problems involving percents.

Isabel got 15 out of 20 questions correct on her math homework. What percent of questions did she get correct?

Write a proportion to find the percent of correct questions:

$$\frac{15}{20} = \frac{n}{100}$$

Cross multiply: $\quad 20n = 1{,}500$

Divide by 20 to find n: $\quad 20n \div 20 = 1{,}500 \div 20$ so $n = 75$

Isabel got 75% of the math questions correct.

Isabel got 80% of the 20 questions on her spelling homework correct. How many questions did she get correct?

Write a proportion to find the number of correct questions:

$$\frac{n}{20} = \frac{80}{100}$$

Cross multiply: $\quad 100n = 1{,}600$

Divide by 100 to find n: $\quad 100n \div 100 = 1{,}600 \div 100$ so $n = 16$

Isabel got 16 spelling questions correct.

Isabel got 90% of the questions on her science homework correct. She got 27 questions correct. How many total science questions were there?

Write a proportion to find the total number of science questions:

$$\frac{27}{n} = \frac{90}{100}$$

Cross multiply: $\quad 90n = 2{,}700$

Divide by 90 to find n: $\quad 90n \div 90 = 2{,}700 \div 90$ so $n = 30$

There were a total of 30 science questions.

UNIT 1
Ratio, Proportion, and Percent

SAMPLE In a 75-minute meeting, 20% of the total time was given to reviewing goals. How many minutes of the meeting were given to reviewing goals?

A   5   B   15   C   20   D   25

The correct answer is B. To find the number of minutes spent reviewing goals, write a proportion. First change 20% to a ratio: $\frac{20}{100}$. So the proportion is $\frac{n}{75} = \frac{20}{100}$. Cross multiply and divide to solve for n: $100n = 1,500$, $100n \div 100 = 1,500 \div 100$, $n = 15$. So 15 minutes were spent reviewing goals.

1 What is 65% of 400?

A   65   C   260

B   215   D   335

2 Doug left $3 as a tip on a lunch bill of $14. Which proportion can be used to find the percent tip Doug left?

A $\frac{3}{14} = \frac{n}{100}$ C $\frac{14}{n} = \frac{3}{100}$

B $\frac{14}{3} = \frac{n}{100}$ D $\frac{n}{14} = \frac{3}{100}$

3 Ten percent of a number equals 40. What is the number?

A   4   C   40

B   14   D   400

4 A realtor gets a 4% commission on the sale of a house. How much commission does the realtor get on the sale of a $180,000 house?

A $4,500   C $45,000

B $7,200   D $72,000

5 This table shows the original price and discount amount of items at a gift store.

Original Price ($)	5	15	25
Discount Amount ($)	1.25	3.75	6.25

Each price in the table is discounted the same percent. What percent is the discount?

A   12.5%   C   50%

B   25%   D   62.5%

6 Forty-eight female students participated in a science fair. This represents 60% of the total students that participated. How many total students participated in the science fair?

A   12   C   80

B   28   D   108

7 A total of 250 tickets to a play were sold. Of those, 210 tickets were sold the week before the play. What percent of tickets were sold the week before the play?

A   46%   C   75%

B   63%   D   84%

SAMPLE Eight new teachers were hired at Plainville Middle School. This represents 16% of the total teachers at the school. How many total teachers are at Plainville Middle School?

Answer _____

To find the total number of teachers, write a proportion: $\frac{8}{n} = \frac{16}{100}$. Cross multiply and divide to solve for *n*: 16*n* = 800, 16*n* ÷ 16 = 800 ÷ 16, *n* = 50. There are a total of 50 teachers at Plainville Middle School.

8 Julia made $200 last week and donated 20% of it to a charity. How much money did she donate?

Answer _____

9 Write a proportion to find what percent 7 is of 28.

Answer _____

10 What is 2% of 44?

Answer _____

11 Tom wrote this proportion to find what number 500 is 85% of.

$$\frac{x}{y} = \frac{z}{100}$$

Which letter represents 500?

Answer _____

12 Marco travels from his house to the beach. The total distance he travels is 120 miles. In the first hour, Marco traveled 54 miles. What percent of the distance did he travel the first hour?

Answer _____

13 A total of 25 students are in German classes. There are 15 students in a beginner German class.

Part A What percent of the total students in the German classes are in the beginner class?

Answer _____

Part B Explain how you used a proportion to find your answer.

_____

_____

_____

14 During a concert, 150 seats in a theater were filled. This represents 75% of the total seats in the theater.

Part A Write a proportion you could use to find the total number of seats.

Answer _____

Part B How many total seats are there? Show your work.

What does the unknown number represent in this proportion?

Answer _____

Types of multi-step percent problems include

  tips
  taxes
  simple interest
  markups and increases
  discounts and decreases

Many multi-step percent problems require you to find the percent of an amount and add or subtract that from the given amount.

The proportion used to find the percent error is

$$\frac{\text{(measured amount – actual amount)}}{\text{actual amount}} = \frac{\text{percent error}}{100}.$$

If the measured amount is less than the actual amount, the percent error will be negative.

Proportions can be used to solve **multi-step percent problems,** that is, problems involving more than one step.

The customer price for books at a bookstore is 40% higher than the price the bookstore owner pays. The bookstore owner pays $12 for a book. What is the customer price for that book?

First find the amount the price of the book is increased. This is 40% of $12.

Write a proportion: $\dfrac{n}{12} = \dfrac{40}{100}$

Cross multiply: $100n = 480$

Divide: $100n \div 100 = 480 \div 100$ so $n = 4.80$

The book price is increased by $4.80. Add this amount to the owner's price to find the customer price.

$$\$12 + \$4.80 = \$16.80$$

The customer price is $16.80.

Use a proportion to find **percent error,** the percent that represents the difference between a measured amount and the actual amount.

Tory finds the mass of an object as 450 grams. The actual mass of the object is 400 grams. What is the percent error in Tory's measurement?

Use a proportion for percent error. The measured amount is 450 grams. The actual amount is 400 grams.

Write a proportion: $\dfrac{(450 - 400)}{400} = \dfrac{n}{100}$

Cross multiply: $400n = 5,000$

Divide: $400n \div 400 = 5,000 \div 400$ so $n = 12.5$

The percent error is 12.5%.

SAMPLE Garrett is paid $300 each week in addition to a sales commission. He earns 3% commission on all his sales. Last week Garrett had $5,000 in sales. How much money did he earn altogether?

    A $150   **B** $450   **C** $800   **D** $1,800

> The correct answer is B. First set up a proportion to find Garrett's commission amount: $\frac{n}{5,000} = \frac{3}{100}$. Solve: $100n = 15,000$, $100n \div 100 = 15,000 \div 100$, $n = 150$. Garrett earned $150 in commission. Now add this amount to his weekly pay to find the total pay: $300 + $150 = $450. Garrett earned a total of $450.

1 Lance paid 6% sales tax on a $30 game. What total amount did Lance pay?

    A $30.60   **C** $33.00

    B $31.80   **D** $36.00

2 Mallory guessed the weight of her dog as 60 pounds. The dog's actual weight is 72 pounds. Which proportion can be used to find the percent error in Mallory's guess?

  A $\dfrac{(72 - 60)}{60} = \dfrac{n}{100}$

  B $\dfrac{(72 - 60)}{72} = \dfrac{n}{100}$

  C $\dfrac{(60 - 72)}{60} = \dfrac{n}{100}$

  D $\dfrac{(60 - 72)}{72} = \dfrac{n}{100}$

3 A sweater is discounted by 20%. The original price of the sweater is $35. What is the discounted price of the sweater?

    A $7   **C** $28

    B $21   **D** $42

4 The population of Springdale increased by 20% in ten years. The population now is 24,000 people. What was the population ten years ago?

    A 14,000   **C** 20,000

    B 19,200   **D** 28,800

5 The sale price of a sofa is $400. The original price was $500. What is the percent discount on the sofa?

    A 10%   **C** 25%

    B 20%   **D** 80%

6 A bank pays 2.5% simple interest each year on savings accounts. Judith puts $600 in her account. How much money will be in this account in one year if no other money is put into the account?

    A $615   **C** $725

    B $625   **D** $750

SAMPLE A credit card company charges a late fee of 10% on all late payments. Last month, Jamal was charged a late fee. The total amount paid, including the late fee, was $275. What was the original amount on the credit card before the late fee?

Answer _____

Let n represent the original amount before the late fee. The proportion $\frac{275 - n}{n} = \frac{10}{100}$ can be used to find this amount. Cross multiply and solve: $100(275 - n) = 10n$

$$27{,}500 - 100n = 10n$$

$$27{,}500 = 110n$$

$$n = 27{,}500 \div 110 = 250$$

The original amount was $250.

7 A savings account now has $2,000 and earns 4% simple interest each year. How much will be in this savings account in a year?

Answer _____

8 Last year, Sheila earned $8.00 an hour. This year, she earns $10.00 an hour. What is the percent increase in the amount Sheila earns?

Answer _____

9 A car dealer discounts the price of a new car by 10%. The discounted price is $16,200. What was the price of the car before the discount?

Answer _____

10 Yesterday, the high temperature was 80° Fahrenheit. Today, the high temperature was 75° Fahrenheit. What is the percent decrease in the high temperatures from yesterday to today?

Answer _____

11 Anthony paid a 20% tip on a $15 dinner bill.

Part A What was the total amount Anthony paid for dinner?

Answer _____

Part B Liam paid a 15% tip on his dinner bill. He left the same dollar amount as a tip that Anthony left. What was the amount of Liam's dinner bill before the tip? Explain how you know.

_____

_____

_____

12 Rihana measured the width of her dining room. Her percent error was −5%. The actual length of her dining room is 120 inches.

Part A What length, in inches, did Rihana measure?

Answer _____

What proportion is used to find the percent error of measurements?

Part B Explain how you found your answer.

_____

_____

_____

_____

REVIEW

Ratio, Proportion, and Percent

Read each problem. Circle the letter of the best answer.

1 Thirty is 60% of what number?

A   18   C   90

B   50   D   180

2 Joe bought 6 jars of sauce for $15. What is the cost for 10 jars of this sauce?

A $19   C $25

B $22   D $30

3 The unit rate for a proportional relationship is 3 miles per hour. Which point must be located on the graph of this proportional relationship?

A   (0, 3)   C   (3, 0)

B   (1, 3)   D   (3, 1)

4 The value of an antique mirror increased by 40% since Juliet bought it. Its value is now $350. What amount did Juliet originally pay for the mirror?

A $140   C $250

B $210   D $310

5 The distance a car travels is proportional to the amount of gas the car uses. The table below shows this relationship.

Distance (mi)	24	40	96
Gas Used (gal)	1.5	2.5	6.0

What is the value of the constant?

A $\frac{1}{16}$ C $\frac{1}{20}$

B   16   D   20

6 A waiting room is $\frac{2}{3}$ full when 36 people are seated. How many people are in the waiting room when it is $\frac{1}{2}$ full?

A   18   C   27

B   24   D   54

7 A printer outputs 30 pages in 120 seconds. Which equation can be used to find the number of pages output, y, in x seconds?

A $y = \frac{1}{4}x$ C $y = 90y$

B $y = 4x$ D $y = 3,600x$

8 Noor rode her bike $\frac{2}{5}$ mile in $\frac{1}{12}$ hour. At this rate, how far would Noor ride her bike in 1 hour?

Answer _____

9 This table shows proportional relationships.

A	9	15	24	36
B	24	40	64	96

What is the ratio that is common throughout this table, written in simplest form?

Answer _____

10 Rosa put $750 into a savings account that earns 3% simple interest each year. She plans to puts no more money into this account. How much money will be in the account in a year?

Answer _____

11 Which pair of x and y quantities in this table are proportional? Write your answer as an ordered pair in the form (x, y).

x	y
10	6
20	16
30	24
40	30
50	36

Answer _____

12 A kitchen scale shows the weight of a piece of fruit is 2 pounds. The actual weight of the fruit is 1.6 pounds. What is the percent error of the kitchen scale?

Answer _____

13 A landscaper charges an hourly rate to do yard work. This afternoon, the landscaper worked 3 hours and was paid $84.

Part A Write an equation that can be used to find *y*, the amount the landscaper gets paid working *x* hours.

Answer _____

Part B The landscaper puts 15% of all his earnings into a savings account. Last month, he worked 100 hours. How much of his earnings last month went into his savings account? Explain how you know.

_____

_____

_____

14 Liz earns 5% commission on all sales she makes. So far this month, she has made $2,400 in sales.

Part A What amount did Liz earn in commission this month?

Answer _____

Part B Liz earns $600 each month in addition to her commission. Last month, she made $8,500 in sales. What was her total monthly pay last month? Explain how you know.

_____

_____

_____

UNIT 2

Operations with Rational Numbers

- **Lesson 1 Adding and Subtracting Rational Numbers** reviews how to add and subtract integers, fractions, mixed numbers, and decimals.

- **Lesson 2 Multiplying and Dividing Rational Numbers** reviews how to multiply and divide integers, fractions, mixed numbers, and decimals.

- **Lesson 3 Operation Properties** reviews the commutative, associative, and distributive properties as well as the identity and inverse properties of addition and multiplication.

- **Lesson 4 Solving Problems with Rational Numbers** reviews how to solve real-world and mathematical problems using the four operations with positive and negative rational numbers.

- **Lesson 5 Estimation** reviews how to use estimation with rational numbers to solve problems and to check the reasonableness of answers.

Adding and Subtracting Rational Numbers

7.NS.1.a–c

A **rational number** is any number that can be written as a fraction. Whole numbers, integers, fractions, and some decimals are rational numbers.

Integers are whole numbers, including 0, and their opposites. A number and its **opposite** are the same distance from 0 on a number line.

–3 and 3 are opposites.

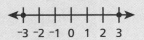

–3 -2 –1 0 1 2 3

The **absolute value** of a number is its distance from 0. The absolute value of any non-zero number is *always* positive.

$$|\text{-}8.15| = 8.15$$

$$\left|\frac{5}{9}\right| = \frac{5}{9}$$

Use the least common multiple (LCM) of unlike denominators as the common denominator.

$$\frac{3}{4} + \frac{1}{6} = \frac{9}{12} + \frac{2}{12} = \frac{11}{12}$$

To add integers with like signs, add their absolute values. The sign of the sum is the same as the sign of the addends.

$$\text{-}2 + (\text{-}3) = |\text{-}2| + |\text{-}3| = 2 + 3 = 5 \rightarrow \text{-}5$$

Both addends are negative, so use the negative sign in the sum: -5

To add integers with different signs, subtract their absolute values. Use the sign of the integer with the larger absolute value for the sum.

$$2 + (\text{-}3) = |2| - |\text{-}3| = 2 - 3 = \text{-}1$$

To subtract integers, rewrite as an addition problem by adding the opposite of the second integer. Then follow the rules for addition.

What is the value of $\text{-}12 - 5$?

Rewrite as an addition problem.
Add the opposite of 5: $\text{-}12 - 5 = \text{-}12 + (\text{-}5)$

Now the integers have like signs.
Add their absolute values: $|\text{-}12| + |\text{-}5| = 12 + 5 = 17$

Both addends are negative, so the sum is -17.

To add or subtract fractions or mixed numbers, first rewrite as equivalent fractions with like denominators. Then add or subtract the numerators. The denominator stays the same.

What is the value of $3\frac{1}{2} + 5\frac{3}{5}$?

Change the mixed numbers to improper fractions: $\frac{7}{2} + \frac{28}{5}$

Rewrite as equivalent fractions
with like denominators: $\frac{7}{2} + \frac{28}{5} = \frac{35}{10} + \frac{56}{10}$

Add. Write the sum as a mixed number: $\frac{35}{10} + \frac{56}{10} = \frac{91}{10} = 9\frac{1}{10}$

To add or subtract decimals, first line up the decimal points. Bring down the decimal point and add or subtract as with whole numbers.

SAMPLE Which expression has the same value as 13 − (−49)?

    A 13 + 49   **B** 13 − 49   **C** −13 + 49   **D** −13 + (−49)

The correct answer is A. Subtracting −49 is the same as adding the opposite of −49. The opposite of −49 is 49, so 13 − (−49) = 13 + 49.

1 Which situation has a result equal to 0?

  A Tim walks 2.3 miles due east and turns around and walks 2.3 miles due west. How far did Tim walk?

  B Mike is 7 years younger than his brother. In 7 years, what will be the age difference between Mike and his brother?

  C Dion opened a checking account and deposited $24.75. He then withdrew $24.75. How much money is left in the checking account?

  D Art is in a hot-air balloon 230 feet off the ground. The balloon climbs another 230 feet. How high off the ground is the hot-air balloon?

2 Which expression is modeled by this number line?

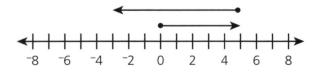

  A −8 − 3 = 5   **C** 3 + 5 = 8

  B −3 + 5 = 8   **D** 5 − 8 = −3

3 Which number line shows the sum of a number and its opposite?

  A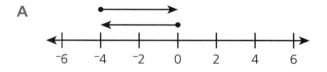

  B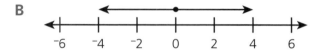

  C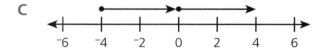

  D

4 Magda's checking account has $42.45. She withdraws $60 from the account. Which equation shows the new balance, in dollars, of Magda's account?

  A 60 − 42.45 = 17.55

  B 60 − 42.45 = 22.55

  C 42.45 − 60 = −17.55

  D 42.45 − 60 = −22.45

SAMPLE The normal body temperature of a horse is about 99.6° Fahrenheit. The normal body temperature of a dog is about 101.3° Fahrenheit. What is the difference between these two normal body temperatures?

Answer _____

> Subtract the two decimals. To do this, first line up the decimal points. Then bring down the decimal point and subtract from right to left. The difference between the temperatures is 1.7° Fahrenheit.

$$\begin{array}{r} \overset{9\,10}{\cancel{10}\,\overset{13}{\cancel{0}}} \\ \cancel{10}\cancel{1}.\cancel{3} \\ -\ 99.6 \\ \hline 1.7 \end{array}$$

5 A submarine starts at sea level and sinks $\frac{1}{5}$ mile. An hour later, it rises $\frac{1}{5}$ mile. What is the depth, in miles, of the submarine after the hour?

Answer _____

6 What is the sum of $\frac{7}{16} + \frac{3}{4}$? Write your answer as a mixed number. Show your work.

Answer _____

7 What is the value of -73 − 36?

Answer _____

8 Show how to find the sum of -5 + 7 on the blank number line below.

What is the sum?

Answer _____

9 Bonnie adds $-2\frac{5}{6}$ and its opposite.

Part A What value results? Explain how you know.

_____

_____

Part B Bonnie subtracts $-2\frac{5}{6}$ from its opposite. Does the same value result as in part A? Explain how you know.

> Write an expression that models this situation. Then find its value.

_____

_____

_____

_____

10 Theo adds -4 and -11.

Part A Draw a model on the number line to show how to find this sum.

What is the sum?

Answer _____

Part B Theo subtracts -4 from -11. Write an equation that shows the difference between these two numbers. Explain how you found the difference.

_____

_____

_____

Multiplying and Dividing Rational Numbers

7.NS.2.a, b, d

To change a rational number written as a fraction to a decimal, divide the numerator by the denominator. The resulting decimal will have either digits that **terminate,** or stop, or digits that repeat.

Terminating Decimal

$$\frac{5}{16} = 0.3125$$

Repeating Decimal

$$\frac{7}{12} = 0.58333\ldots$$

The symbol … indicates repeating digits.

To multiply decimals, first multiply as you do whole numbers. Then count the number of digits to the right of the decimal point in each number. This is the same as the number of digits to the right of the decimal point in the answer.

To multiply fractions, first multiply the numerators. Then multiply the denominators. Simplify the product if possible. To divide fractions, rewrite as a multiplication expression. To do this, multiply by the **reciprocal,** or inverse, of the second fraction.

What is the quotient of $\frac{5}{6} \div \frac{2}{3}$?

Rewrite using multiplication: $\frac{5}{6} \div \frac{2}{3} = \frac{5}{6} \times \frac{3}{2}$

Multiply and simplify: $\frac{5}{6} \times \frac{3}{2} = \frac{15}{12} = \frac{5}{4}$

Write as a mixed number: $\frac{5}{4} = 1\frac{1}{4}$

The quotient is $\frac{5}{4}$ or $1\frac{1}{4}$.

The process used to multiply or divide decimals is like the process used for whole numbers. However, the placement of the decimal in the answer follows certain rules.

What is the value of 6.25 ÷ 0.5?

Write the division expression vertically: $0.5\overline{)6.25}$

Move the decimal point in the divisor to the right to make it a whole number. Move the decimal point in the dividend the same number of places to the right.

$0.5\overline{)6.25} = 5\overline{)62.5}$

Divide as you do whole numbers. Put the decimal point in the quotient directly above the decimal point in the dividend.

The value of 6.25 ÷ 0.5 is 12.5.

$$
\begin{array}{r}
12.5 \\
5\overline{)62.5} \\
\underline{5} \\
12 \\
\underline{10} \\
2\,5 \\
\underline{2\,5} \\
0
\end{array}
$$

SAMPLE The quotient of $2\frac{3}{5} \div 1\frac{1}{5}$ is $\frac{13}{6}$. Which of the following is **not** the quotient of $2\frac{3}{5} \div \left(-1\frac{1}{5}\right)$?

A $-\frac{13}{6}$ B $\frac{-13}{6}$ C $\frac{-13}{-6}$ D $\frac{13}{-6}$

The correct answer is C. Since the signs of each number in the division expression are different, the quotient will be negative. The fractions in choices A, B, and D are all negative since they each have one negative sign. The quotient in choice C, however, is positive since there are two negative signs. In division, two negatives result in a positive quotient.

1 Which product is negative?

A $7.2 \times (-2.75)$ C $-87 \times (-13)$

B $-3\frac{4}{9} \times 0$ D $\frac{-7}{-8} \times 2.6$

2 Which number forms a repeating decimal?

A $\frac{3}{8}$ C $1\frac{1}{4}$

B $\frac{12}{10}$ D $3\frac{5}{6}$

3 What is the value of the expression below?

$$-1.6 \times (-25)$$

A 4.0   C −40

B 40   D −400

4 Which number is equal to $-\frac{7}{10} \times \left(-\frac{2}{3}\right)$?

A $\frac{-7}{15}$ C 0.466

B $-\frac{7}{15}$ D 0.466…

5 What is the product of $2\frac{3}{4}$ and $1\frac{1}{3}$?

A $2\frac{1}{4}$ C 3.66

B $3\frac{2}{3}$ D 4.0833

6 Which of the following equations is true?

A $\frac{0}{-6} = -6$ C $\frac{-36}{-4} = -9$

B $-\frac{15}{0} = 0$ D $\frac{60}{-5} = -12$

7 Which quotient results in a terminating decimal?

A $\frac{5}{6} \div \frac{1}{3}$ C $\frac{1}{2} \div \frac{3}{5}$

B $50 \div \frac{6}{5}$ D $100 \div \frac{3}{4}$

SAMPLE Is the quotient of $-15.375 \div 0$ equal to 0, a positive rational number, a negative rational number, or neither? Explain how you know.

Answer _____

 It is not possible to divide by 0, so there is no quotient for this expression. There is no number that can be multiplied by 0 to equal -15.375. Therefore there is no number that is the quotient of dividing by 0. Division by 0 is said to be undefined.

8 What is the value of $\frac{3}{8} \div 6$?

Answer _____

9 Juan thinks the product of $(-2)(-5)(-4)(-3)$ is positive. Leon thinks it is negative. Who is correct? Explain how you know.

_____

_____

_____

10 Are the values of $\frac{-3}{0}$ and $\frac{0}{-3}$ the same? Explain how you know.

_____

_____

_____

11 Write a division expression that is equivalent to $\frac{8}{15} \times \left(-\frac{3}{5}\right)$.

Answer _____

12 Manny wrote the expression $8\frac{1}{4} \div (-4)$.

Part A Write two different expressions that are equivalent to this.

Answer 1 _____

Answer 2 _____

Part B What is the value of these expressions? Show your work.

Answer _____

13 Lila multiplied $\frac{-2}{5}$ by itself.

Part A What product did Lila get? Write your answer as a fraction.

What does it mean to multiply a number by itself?

Answer _____

Part B Write an equation equivalent to this using decimals.

Answer _____

Operation Properties

7.NS.1.d, 7.NS.2.c

The **zero product property** says that when you multiply any number by 0, the result will be 0.

$-2.78 \times 0 = 0$

The commutative and associative properties do not apply to subtraction or division.

The distributive property also applies to multiplication over subtraction.

$a(b - c) = ab - ac$
$2(6 - 1) = 2(6) - 2(1)$
$2(5) = 12 - 2$
$10 = 10$

The **additive identity** is 0.

The **multiplicative identity** is 1.

The **additive inverse** of a number is its opposite.

The **multiplicative inverse** of a number is its reciprocal.

Operation properties allow you to write equivalent expressions in different forms.

The **commutative property** says you can add or multiply two numbers in any order and the result will be the same.

$$a + b = b + a \quad a \cdot b = b \cdot a$$
$$3 + 6 = 6 + 3 \quad 3 \cdot 6 = 6 \cdot 3$$

The **associative property** says you can use parentheses to group three numbers together in any order when you add or multiply and the result will be the same.

$$a + (b + c) = (a + b) + c \quad a \cdot (b \cdot c) = (a \cdot b) \cdot c$$
$$7 + (3 + 4) = (7 + 3) + 4 \quad 7 \cdot (3 \cdot 4) = (7 \cdot 3) \cdot 4$$
$$7 + 7 = 10 + 4 \quad 7 \cdot (12) = (21) \cdot 4$$
$$14 = 14 \quad 84 = 84$$

The **distributive property** says you can multiply the sum of two numbers or you can multiply each addend separately and then add the products. The result will be the same.

$$a \cdot (b + c) = a \cdot b + a \cdot c$$
$$2 \cdot (6 + 1) = 2 \cdot 6 + 2 \cdot 1$$
$$2 \cdot (7) = 12 + 2$$
$$14 = 14$$

The **identity property** says you can either add 0 to any number or multiply any number by 1 and the number will stay the same.

$$n + 0 = n \quad n \cdot 1 = n$$
$$5 + 0 = 5 \quad 9 \cdot 1 = 9$$

The **inverse property** says that the sum of a number and its inverse is 0 or the product of a number and its inverse is 1.

$$n + (-n) = 0 \quad n \cdot \frac{1}{n} = 1$$

$$8 + (-8) = 0 \quad 3 \cdot \frac{1}{3} = 1$$

SAMPLE Jin Mei wrote the equation $-\frac{2}{5} \cdot \square = 1$. What number goes in the box to make the number sentence true?

A $\frac{2}{5}$ B $-\frac{3}{5}$ C $-\frac{5}{2}$ D $\frac{7}{5}$

The correct answer is C. The inverse property of multiplication says that the product of any number and its reciprocal is 1. The sign of any number and its reciprocal are the same. The reciprocal of $-\frac{2}{5}$ is $-\frac{5}{2}$.

1 Which property is shown by the equation below?

$$\frac{3}{8} + \left(\frac{1}{4} + \frac{5}{6}\right) = \left(\frac{3}{8} + \frac{1}{4}\right) + \frac{5}{6}$$

A commutative C distributive

B associative D identity

2 Which of the following equations is true?

A $9 - 5 = 5 - 9$

B $(7 - 1) + 4 = (7 - 4) + 1$

C $(6 - 3) - 2 = 6 - (3 - 2)$

D $3 \times (8 - 5) = 3 \times 8 - 3 \times 5$

3 Jared multiplies $\frac{1}{2}$ by a number, n, and the product is 1. What is n?

A $\frac{1}{2}$ C 2

B $-\frac{1}{2}$ D -2

4 Which equation shows an example of the zero product property?

A $\frac{0}{4} \times \frac{5}{0} = 0$

B $-\frac{4}{5} \times \left(-\frac{5}{4}\right) = 1$

C $-4.5 + 4.5 = 0$

D $-4.5 \times 4.5 \times 0 = 0$

5 Which property is shown by the equation below?

$(9.76 \times 3.1) \times 6.5 = 6.5 \times (9.76 \times 3.1)$

A commutative C distributive

B associative D identity

6 Which expression has the same value as $(-8) \times 75$?

A $-8 \times 70 \cdot 5$ C $-8 \cdot (70 + 5)$

B $-8 \times 70 + 5$ D $-8 + (70 \times 5)$

SAMPLE Rewrite the expression below to show the commutative property of multiplication.

$$2 \times (5 \times 7)$$

Answer _____

The commutative property of multiplication says that two numbers can be multiplied in any order and the result will be the same. Since $5 \times 7 = 7 \times 5$, the expression can be rewritten as $2 \times (7 \times 5)$. Similarly, the product 5×7 inside the parentheses can be treated as one factor and 2 as the other factor. So, the expression can also be rewritten as $(5 \times 7) \times 2$.

7 What value of n makes the equation below true?

$$-\frac{8}{3} + n = 0$$

Answer _____

8 What property is shown by the equation $-0.6 + 0.6 = 0$?

Answer _____

9 Nelson thinks the equation $10 \times \frac{1}{10} = 1$ shows the multiplication identity property. Is he correct? Explain how you know.

_____

_____

_____

10 Lakshmi wrote the equation $5 + (-9 + 6) = 5 + (6 - 9)$. Is this equation true? Explain how you know.

_____

_____

_____

UNIT 2 ▨▨▨▨▨▨▨▨▨▨▨▨▨▨▨▨▨▨▨▨▨▨▨▨▨▨▨▨▨
Operations with Rational Numbers

11 Maxwell wrote the expression 6 × 18.

    Part A Rewrite this expression using the commutative property.

        Answer _____

    Part B Rewrite the expression 6 × 18 two different ways to show the distributive property over both addition and subtraction.

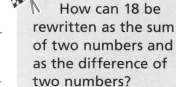

How can 18 be rewritten as the sum of two numbers and as the difference of two numbers?

        Answer 1 _____

        Answer 2 _____

12 The equation below is **not** true.

$$(50 \div 10) \times 2 = 50 \div (10 \times 2)$$

    Part A Explain why the equation is not true.

_____

_____

_____

    Part B Rewrite the equation so that it is true.

        Answer _____

Solving Problems with Rational Numbers

7.NS.3, 7.EE.3

LESSON 4

Sometimes key words give clues as to what operation to use. Some key words are

(+) add
  sum
  increased by
  more than
  altogether

(−) subtract
  difference
  fewer
  less than
  decreased by
  how many more
  how many are left

(×) multiply
  product
  groups of
  in all
  of

(÷) divide
  quotient
  groups of
  shared equally

In multi-step word problems, be sure to perform each operation in the correct order.

To solve word problems involving rational numbers, you need to decide which operations to use. Some word problems involve using only one operation.

Maura got a 30% discount on a rug. The original price of the rug was $129. What was the total amount of the discount?

To find the amount of the discount, multiply 139 by 30%.

$$139 \times 30\% = 139 \times 0.30 = 41.7$$

The amount of the discount was $41.70.

Other word problems involve using more than one operation.

Maura wants to center the rug in her living room. The rug is $8\frac{3}{4}$ feet wide. The total width of her living room is $12\frac{1}{2}$ feet. How far from each wall of her living room should Maura place the rug?

First find the width of the room that will not be covered by the rug. To do this, subtract.

$$12\frac{1}{2} - 8\frac{3}{4} = \frac{25}{2} - \frac{35}{4} = \frac{50}{4} - \frac{35}{4} = \frac{15}{4} = 3\frac{3}{4} \text{ feet}$$

Next, divide this amount by 2 since the rug will be centered.

$$3\frac{3}{4} \div 2 = \frac{15}{4} \times \frac{1}{2} = \frac{15}{8} = 1\frac{7}{8} \text{ feet}$$

The rug should be placed $1\frac{7}{8}$ feet from each wall.

UNIT 2
Operations with Rational Numbers

SAMPLE Nathan bought 2 sandwiches and a beverage. Each sandwich cost $4.75. The beverage cost $1.29. How much change should Nathan get back if he pays with a $20 bill?

A $9.21   B $9.79   C $10.21   D $10.79

   The correct answer is A. First find the total cost of the sandwiches and beverage. Multiply the cost of the sandwich by 2. Then add the cost of the beverage: $4.75 × 2 = $9.50, $9.50 + $1.29 = $10.79. Then subtract the total cost from $20 to find the amount of change: $20.00 − $10.79 = $9.21.

1 On June 1, Tiffany's bank account had -$55.72. On June 30, it had -$8.09. Which expression could be used to find the change in value?

A   -55.72 + (-8.09)   C   -8.09 − 55.72

B   -55.72 − (-8.09)   D   -8.09 − (-55.72)

2 Nobu filled a $1\frac{1}{2}$-cup measuring cup $3\frac{1}{2}$ times. How many cups of water is this?

A $3\frac{1}{4}$ C $5\frac{1}{4}$

B   5   D   5.14

3 A new computer costs $800. So far Meg has saved $350. She wants to know how much she should save each month in order to get the computer in 12 months. Which operations should be used to solve this problem?

A   subtraction and division

B   addition and subtraction

C   addition and multiplication

D   subtraction and multiplication

4 A car can travel 21 miles on each gallon of gas. Its gas tank holds 13.7 gallons. How many miles can the car travel on one tank of gas?

A   213.7   C   287.7

B   273.7   D   321.7

5 The monthly membership fee at a gym increased by 10% this year. Last year, the cost of a monthly membership was $28.50. What is the total yearly cost for a membership at the gym this year?

A $307.80   C $334.20

B $319.20   D $376.20

6 Paloma averaged a time of 2.3 minutes in each lap of a race. Marissa averaged 2.75 minutes in each lap. There were a total of 4 laps in the race. How many minutes ahead of Marissa did Paloma finish the race?

A   0.45   C   2.8

B   1.8   D   4.45

SAMPLE Karen has 48 inches of ribbon. She wants to place the ribbon along the edge of a rectangular frame that is 12 inches wide and 16 inches long. Will Karen have enough ribbon or will she need more? Explain how you know.

Answer _____

First find the total amount of ribbon Karen will need. To do this, add the length and width of the rectangle and then multiply by 2 since a rectangle has 2 lengths and 2 widths: 12 + 16 = 28, 28 × 2 = 56 inches needed. Then subtract the amount needed from the amount she has: 48 − 56 = -8. The negative result means Karen does not have enough ribbon. She will need 8 more inches.

7 School lunch costs $2.75. What is the total cost of 5 school lunches?

Answer _____

8 A bag of trail mix weighs $11\frac{1}{2}$ ounces. Each serving of trail mix is $\frac{3}{4}$ ounce. How many servings are in the bag of trail mix? Show your work.

Answer _____

9 The outside temperature at 6:00 A.M. one day was -2.4°C. The temperature dropped 0.8°C each hour for the next 4 hours. What was the outside temperature after the 4 hours? Show your work.

Answer _____

10 A shoe store advertises this special.

Shoe Special

Buy one pair of shoes,
get the second pair for

$\frac{1}{2}$ **off!**

Second pair must be equal to
or less than the cost of the first pair.

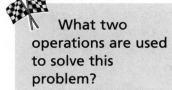

What two operations are used to solve this problem?

Part A Willie buys two pairs of shoes. They both cost $55. What is his total cost for both pairs? Explain how you found your answer.

_____

_____

_____

Part B Antonia spends $65 for two pairs of shoes. The more expensive pair cost $45. What was the original cost of the other pair? Explain how you know.

_____

_____

_____

Estimation

7.EE.3

To round a number, look at the digit to the right of the place being rounded to. If the digit is 5 or more, round up. Otherwise, round down.

Compatible numbers are a set of numbers that are easy to compute with. They are not always the closest values a number rounds to.

45 and 5 are compatible for division since 5 evenly divides 45.

To estimate with percents, round to a more common percent. Some common percents and their values are

$$10\% = 0.1 = \frac{1}{10}$$

$$25\% = 0.25 = \frac{1}{4}$$

$$33\% \approx 0.33 \approx \frac{1}{3}$$

$$50\% = 0.5 = \frac{1}{2}$$

$$66\% \approx 0.67 \approx \frac{2}{3}$$

$$75\% = 0.75 = \frac{3}{4}$$

To **estimate** an answer is to find its approximate value. You can use estimation to predict the answers to word problems. Some strategies for estimating include rounding numbers or finding compatible numbers. This can help you approximate calculations mentally.

A marathon is 26.2 miles long. Dylan runs an average of 1 mile in 7.5 minutes. Estimate the number of minutes Dylan will take to run the entire marathon at this rate.

Round each measurement using compatible numbers.

26.2 rounds down to 25 and 7.5 rounds up to 8.

Multiply using the compatible numbers.

$$25 \times 8 = 200$$

Dylan will take about 200 minutes to run this marathon.

You can also use estimation to check the reasonableness of calculations.

Rita will buy a new computer monitor that costs $409. The sales tax rate in her state is 2.9%. She calculates the sales tax on this computer monitor as $11.86. Is Rita's calculation reasonable?

Round the cost of the monitor and the sales tax rate.

$409 rounds to $400. 2.9% rounds to 3%.

Multiply the rounded amounts.

$$\$400 \times 3\% = \$400 \times 0.03 = \$12$$

$12 is close in value to $11.86, so yes, Rita's calculation is reasonable.

SAMPLE Henry will buy grass seed for his lawn. Each bag of grass seed covers an area of 925 square feet. Henry's lawn is 128 feet long and 72 feet wide. He estimates that he will need 8 bags of grass seed. Is this estimate reasonable?

   A Yes, 8 bags is a reasonable estimate.

   B No, 6 bags is a more reasonable estimate.

   C No, 10 bags is a more reasonable estimate.

   D No, 12 bags is a more reasonable estimate.

> The correct answer is C. To estimate the total number of bags needed, first round the given measurements: 128 rounds to 130 and 72 rounds to 70. Next find the approximate area of the lawn: 130 × 70 = 9,100 square feet. Then divide the area of the lawn by the area covered in each bag: 925 rounds to 900, and 9,100 ÷ 900 is approximately 10. So 10 bags is more reasonable.

1 Which of the following compatible numbers can be used to best estimate the value of the expression below?

$$122 \div 24$$

   A 100 ÷ 25   **C** 125 ÷ 25

   B 120 ÷ 20   **D** 150 ÷ 20

2 A day on Earth lasts 24 hours. A day on Venus lasts 243 Earth days. Which is a reasonable estimate for the number of hours in one day on Venus?

   A 10   **C** 4,000

   B 2,000   **D** 6,000

3 In a survey of 634 workers, about 18.6% of them take longer than 45 minutes to drive to work. Courtney calculates that 62 workers take longer than 45 minutes to drive to work. Is her calculation reasonable?

   A Yes, because 10% of 600 is 60.

   B No, because 10% of 700 is 70.

   C No, because 20% of 600 is 120.

   D No, because 20% of 700 is 140.

4 The population of the United States is approximately 310,142,000. The population of Texas is approximately 12.4% of this total. What is a reasonable estimate for the population of Texas?

   A 12,000,000   **C** 30,000,000

   B 20,000,000   **D** 45,000,000

SAMPLE Ryan works 37.5 hours a week. His yearly salary is $33,846. Ryan gets paid to work 52 weeks a year. What is a reasonable estimate for the dollar amount he gets paid each hour?

Answer _____

First estimate the total number of hours he works a year. Round and multiply the weekly hours by the number of hours a week he works: 37.5 rounds up to 40 and 52 rounds down to 50, and 40 × 50 = 2,000 hours. Next, round his annual salary and divide by the estimated total hours: $33,846 rounds down to $30,000, and 30,000 ÷ 2,000 = 15. Ryan gets paid about $15 an hour.

5 A field has an area of $7,363\frac{1}{8}$ square feet. The width of the field is $62\frac{1}{4}$ feet. Estimate the length of this field.

Answer _____

6 What is a reasonable estimate for the value of the expression below?

$$-26.3125 + 8.75 - (-48.375)$$

Answer _____

7 The regular rate for a hotel room is $248 a night. The hotel also charges an 11.7% room tax. What is a reasonable estimate for the total cost of the hotel room, including tax, for one night?

Answer _____

8 The side lengths of a triangle, in inches, are $18\frac{3}{4}$, $27\frac{7}{12}$, and $12\frac{1}{3}$. Paula calculates the total distance around this triangle as $58\frac{2}{3}$ inches. Is her calculation reasonable? Explain how you know.

_____

_____

_____

9 The list below shows the items on Alexa's shopping list and the cost for each item.

- 4 cans of soup: $2.39 each
- 2 boxes of cereal: $4.19 each
- $1\frac{1}{2}$ pounds of cheese: $6.79 per pound

Part A Alexa buys these items with a $50 bill. What is a reasonable estimate for the amount of change she should get back?

> Don't forget to include all the items Alexa bought.
> About how much do 4 cans of soup cost?

Answer _____

Part B Explain how you found your estimate.

_____

_____

_____

10 A contractor charges $14.60 per square foot to build a deck. Jody wants to have a rectangular deck built that is 16 feet long and 18 feet wide.

Part A Jody estimates the total charge from this contractor to be $3,000. Is her estimate reasonable?

Answer _____

Part B Explain how you know your answer is correct.

_____

_____

_____

REVIEW

Operations with Rational Numbers

Read each problem. Circle the letter of the best answer.

1 Which quotient is positive?

A $0 \div \frac{2}{5}$

C $14 \div (-6)$

B $-0.2 \div 3$

D $\frac{-4}{3} \div \left(-1\frac{5}{6}\right)$

2 Which number line models the equation $-3 - (-5)$?

A
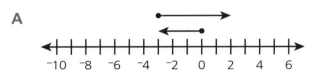

B
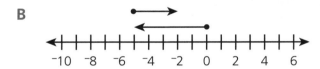

C
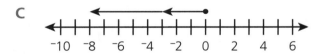

D
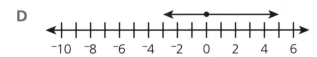

3 Alison walked 0.4 mile due south. Then she walked 0.4 mile due north. What number represents Alison's total distance from her starting point?

A   0

C   -0.4

B   0.4

D   0.8

4 A submarine was at a depth of -40 feet. An hour later, it was at a depth of -85 feet. Which expression represents the submarine's change in depth in that hour?

A $-40 - 85$

C $-85 - 40$

B $-40 + 85$

D $-85 + 40$

5 Kathy is painting the outside of her house. Its area is 2,250 square feet. Each gallon of paint covers 250 square feet and costs $19.90. What is the least the paint will cost?

A $139.30

C $199.00

B $179.10

D $258.70

6 Which number equals $-3\frac{1}{2} \times \left(-2\frac{2}{3}\right)$?

A   6.33

C   9.33…

B   -6.33…

D   -9.33

7 Which of the following equations is true?

A $12 \div 6 = 6 \div 12$

B $(8 \times 5) \times 2 = 2 \times (8 \times 5)$

C $10 \times (3 + 9) = 10 \times 3 + 9$

D $(20 \div 4) \div 2 = 20 \div (4 \div 2)$

8 Fish costs $6.40 per pound. Jordan bought some fish that cost a total of $23.20. How many pounds of fish did he buy?

Answer _____

9 What is the sum of $\frac{5}{6} + \frac{7}{8}$? Write your answer as a mixed number. Show your work.

Answer _____

10 Bart cut a $4\frac{1}{3}$-foot board into 3 equal pieces. How long is each piece?

Answer _____

11 Is the product of the expression below positive or negative? Explain how you know.

$$-(-0.725)(3.25)(4.4)$$

_____

_____

12 Does the equation $5 + 0 = 5$ show the additive inverse property? Explain how you know.

_____

_____

13 When Olivia started a business, the amount of profit she had was -$1,550. During the first 6 months, her profit increased by $250 each month. What was the amount of Olivia's profit at the end of the first 6 months?

Answer _____

14 Reilly divided $-\frac{5}{4}$ by its reciprocal.

Part A What quotient did Reilly get? Write your answer as a fraction.

Answer _____

Part B Write an equation equivalent to this using decimals.

Answer _____

15 Mikayla's class is going on a field trip to a museum.

- Tickets to the museum cost $9.50 per person.
- A total of 58 people are going.
- Transportation to the museum costs a total of $139.

Part A Mikayla calculates the total cost of the museum trip as $690. Is her calculation reasonable?

Answer _____

Part B Explain how you know.

_____

_____

_____

UNIT

3

Expressions

- ● **Lesson 1 Writing Expressions** reviews how to represent situations using algebraic expressions and shows how more than one expression can represent a situation.

- ● **Lesson 2 Simplifying Expressions** reviews how to simplify algebraic expressions by using the distributive property and by combining like terms.

- ● **Lesson 3 Adding and Subtracting Expressions** reviews how to combine expressions using addition or subtraction.

- ● **Lesson 4 Factoring Expressions** reviews how to factor an expression using its greatest common factor.

Writing Expressions

7.EE.2

An **expression** is a grouping of numbers and operations that show the value of something. An **algebraic expression** is an expression that also contains variables. A **variable** is a symbol or letter that represents an unknown value or a value that can change.

An algebraic expression represents a number.

Some examples of algebraic expressions include

$$x + 3 \qquad m + n \qquad \frac{-2}{y - 7} \qquad p^2 + 4p$$

You can translate words into algebraic expressions. Some examples are

Expression	Meaning
$x + 1$	One more than a number
$x - 6$	Six less than a number
$5 - x$	A number less than five
$2x$	Twice a number
$\frac{x}{4}$	A number divided by four
$\frac{2}{3}x - 7$	Seven less than two-thirds a number

A variable can be a symbol or a letter of the alphabet. Some variables include _a, d, n, p, x,_ and _y._

A variable can represent any number.

You can rewrite expressions to have the same value. These are called **equivalent expressions.**

A store is having a going-out-of-business sale. All items are 30% off. Write an expression that shows the percent of the original price, _x_, of each item a customer pays.

Use subtraction to represent a decrease in price.

$$x - 0.30x$$

This expression shows that 0.30, or 30%, of the original price is subtracted from the original price.

$$x - 0.30x = 0.70x$$

This means that a customer pays 0.70, or 70%, of the original price. The expressions $x - 0.30x$ and $0.70x$ are equivalent.

Many different expressions can be written that are equivalent to each other.

Some equivalent expressions for _3n_ are

$$n + n + n$$

$$-2n + 5n$$

$$3 + 3n - 3$$

$$\frac{12n}{4}$$

SAMPLE Tammy has 80 trading cards that she will share among some friends. Each friend will get the same number of trading cards. Which expression represents the number of trading cards each friend will get?

A $\frac{n}{80}$ **B** $\frac{80}{n}$ **C** $n - 80$ **D** $80 - n$

The correct answer is B. Division is the operation used to represent items that are shared equally. The total number of cards is divided by the number of friends. Here, the variable n represents the number of friends. The numerator is the total number of cards, 80, and the denominator is the number of friends, n, sharing the cards.

1 Which expression is equivalent to the one shown below?

$$6y - 3 + y$$

A $3y$ **C** $6 - 3y$

B $3 + y$ **D** $7y - 3$

2 Tran has c coins. Each coin is worth 50 cents. Which expression shows the value of these coins, in cents?

A $50c$ **C** $c \div 50$

B $c + 50$ **D** $50 - c$

3 Which expression represents the quotient of 6 and a number k?

A $6k$ **C** $k \div 6$

B $6 - k$ **D** $6 \div k$

4 Kate is 7 years older than Ginger. If Kate is x years old, which expression represents Ginger's age?

A $7x$ **C** $x - 7$

B $7 + x$ **D** $7 - x$

5 Josh bought some boxes of fruit snacks, containing 8 pouches each. He gave 4 pouches to friends. Which expression shows the number of pouches of fruit snacks Josh has left?

A $4p - 8$ **C** $4 - 8p$

B $8p - 4$ **D** $8 - 4p$

6 Caroline got some goldfish. Her sister got 3 less than twice as many goldfish as Caroline. Which expression shows the total number of goldfish Caroline and her sister got?

A $3 - g$ **C** $3 - 2g$

B $2g - 3$ **D** $3g - 3$

7 A pizza is cut into p equal-sized pieces. Max ate 3 pieces. Antwon and Carlos both ate 2 pieces. Which expression shows the fraction of pieces left?

A $\frac{p}{5}$ **C** $\frac{7}{p}$

B $\frac{p - 5}{5}$ **D** $\frac{p - 7}{p}$

SAMPLE The area of a rectangle equals its length times its width. The length of a certain rectangle is 8 more than one-fourth its width. Write an expression that shows the area of this rectangle.

Answer _____

Let the variable w represent the unknown width of the rectangle. "The length is 8 more than one-fourth its width" can be translated as $\frac{1}{4}w + 8$, so the expression for the area of the rectangle is $\left(\frac{1}{4}w + 8\right)w$.

8 Write an expression to represent the quotient of 9 and the difference of a number and 5.

Answer _____

9 Nicole used q quarters in a parking meter. Ashley used 6 less than 3 times the number of quarters Nicole used. Write an expression that represents the number of quarters Ashley used.

Answer _____

10 Brendan earns 25% more than his regular hourly rate, d, when he works on holidays. Write an expression to represent the hourly rate Brendan earns working on a holiday.

Answer _____

11 Is a number less than 10 the same as the difference of a number and 10? Explain how you know.

_____

_____

12 Jeremy is 4 inches shorter than Kevin. Kevin is *n* inches tall.

Part A Write an expression to represent Jeremy's height.

Answer _____

Part B Dimitri is 3 inches taller than Jeremy. Write an expression to represent Dimitri's height. Use the expression to explain how Dimitri's height compares to Kevin's height.

_____

_____

_____

13 In a gift shop, magnets cost $4.50 each and postcards cost $0.75 each.

Part A Marisol bought the same number of magnets as postcards in this gift shop. Write an expression to show her total cost.

Answer _____

> **What expression could represent the cost of the magnets? What expression could represent the cost of the postcards?**

Part B Write another expression equivalent to the one you wrote in part A. Explain why both expressions are correct.

_____

_____

_____

_____

Simplifying Expressions

7.EE.1

To combine like terms, combine the **coefficients,** or numbers that are in front of the variables. The variable part stays the same.

$$6y + 3y = 9y$$

Commutative Property:
$$a + b = b + a$$
$$ab = ba$$

Distributive Property:
$$a(b + c) = ab + bc$$

If a variable term has no number in front, the number 1 can be used without changing its value.

$$7 + t + 3t =$$
$$7 + 1t + 3t =$$
$$7 + 4t$$

Be sure to distribute any negative signs.

$$3m - (m + 4) =$$
$$3m - 1(m + 4) =$$
$$3m - 1m - 4 =$$
$$2m - 4$$

Expressions are made up of **terms,** or groups of numbers and variables, separated by addition. The expression $4x - 3y^2 - x + 7$ has the terms $4x$, $-3y^2$, $-x$, and 7. **Like terms** are terms that have the same variable parts.

> $4x$ and $-x$ are like terms.
> $-3y^2$, $-x$, and 7 are unlike terms.

An expression can be simplified by combining like terms.

> Simplify the expression $3x^2 - 5xy + 2y^2 + 8xy$.

> Rewrite using the commutative property and combine like terms. The like terms are $-5xy$ and $8xy$.

$$3x^2 - 5xy + 2y^2 + 8xy = 3x^2 - 5xy + 8xy + 2y^2$$
$$= 3x^2 + 3xy + 2y^2$$

> Unlike terms stay the same.

$$3x^2 - 5xy + 2y^2 + 8xy = 3x^2 + 3xy + 2y^2$$

Sometimes you can simplify an expression by using the distributive property.

> Simplify the expression $4(a - 3b) - 5a + 2$.

> Apply the distributive property to remove the parentheses.

$$4(a - 3b) - 5a + 2 = 4a - 12b - 5a + 2$$

> Rewrite using the commutative property and combine like terms. The like terms are $4a$ and $-5a$.

$$4a - 12b - 5a + 2 = 4a - 5a - 12b + 2$$
$$= -a - 12b + 2$$

> Unlike terms stay the same.

$$4(a - 3b) - 5a + 2 = -a - 12b + 2$$

SAMPLE Which expression is equivalent to the expression $5(x + 1) - 2(x - 3)$?

A $3x - 1$ B $3x - 2$ C $3x + 1$ D $3x + 11$

The correct answer is D. Use the distributive property to remove the parentheses. Be sure to multiply all terms in the second set of parentheses by -2. This gives $5x + 5 - 2x + 6$. Combining like terms gives $3x + 11$.

1 What are the like terms in the expression below?

$$8k + 6k^2 - 2k - 2$$

A $8k$ and $-2k$

B $-2k$ and -2

C $8k$, $6k^2$, and $-2k$

D $8k$, $6k^2$, $-2k$, and -2

2 Simplify $6r + 3(2r + 1)$.

A $11r + 1$ C $12r + 1$

B $11r + 3$ D $12r + 3$

3 What is the simplified form of the expression $6 - 2w - w$?

A $3w$ C $6 - w$

B $4w - 1$ D $6 - 3w$

4 Which expression is already in its simplified form?

A $3t + (s + t)$

B $6h + 2(h + 3k)$

C $5m + 7mn + 4n$

D $8 + y^3 - 5z^2 + 2y^3$

5 Simplify this expression.

$$12p - 7p - 3q - q$$

A $5p - 2q$ C $5p^2 - 2q^2$

B $5p - 4q$ D $5p^2 - 4q^2$

6 Simplify this expression.

$$g - 3(f - g) - 2f$$

A $-f$ C $-2g - 5f$

B $-5f$ D $4g - 5f$

7 Simplify $5v(3 + w) - (v + 2w)$.

A $14v - w$

B $15v + 3vw$

C $14v + 5vw - 2w$

D $15v + 4vw + 2w$

8 The perimeter of a rectangle equals the sum of twice its length and twice its width. A rectangle has a length of $4n + 3$ units and a width of $3n$ units. Write an expression for the perimeter of this rectangle in simplest form.

A $7n + 3$ C $14n + 6$

B $7n + 6$ D $14n + 12$

SAMPLE Are the expressions below equivalent? Explain how you know.

$$2d - (c - 3d) \text{ and } 4c - 5(c - d)$$

Answer _____

Use the distributive property to simplify each expression:
$$2d - (c - 3d) = 2d - c + 3d = 5d - c$$
$$4c - 5(c - d) = 4c - 5c + 5d = \text{-}c + 5d$$

By the commutative property, $5d - c = \text{-}c + 5d$. Yes, the expressions are equivalent.

9 Write this expression in simplest form. Show your work.

$$4(z - 1) + 2(3z + 2)$$

Answer _____

10 Elizabeth simplified the expression $5x - 3(4 - x)$ and got $2x - 12$. Did she simplify the expression correctly? Explain how you know.

_____

_____

11 Are the expressions $5x + 3xy - 5x$ and $7xy - 4y$ equivalent? Explain how you know.

_____

_____

12 Look at this expression.

$$5x^2 + 2x + 4xy - 3x^2 - 7x + 3y$$

Part A Which terms are like terms?

Answer _____

_____

Is there more than one set of like terms in this expression?

Part B What is the simplified form of this expression? Explain how you found your answer.

_____

_____

_____

_____

13 Brenda wrote the expression $8n + 3(n - 2) - 6n - 1$.

Part A What is the simplified form of this expression?

Answer _____

Part B Write an expression equivalent to the one you wrote in part A that has exactly 4 terms.

Answer _____

Adding and Subtracting Expressions

7.EE.1

You can also add expressions by first aligning like terms vertically.

$$6x^2 + 5x - 3$$
$$+ \; x^2 \qquad - 9$$

Commutative Property of Addition:

$$a + b = b + a$$

Associative Property of Addition:

$$a + (b + c) = (a + b) + c$$

Adding the opposite of each term in the second expression is like multiplying each term in that expression by -1.

$$-(p + 4) =$$
$$-1(p + 4) =$$
$$-1 \cdot p + -1 \cdot 4 =$$
$$-p - 4$$

You can simplify algebraic expressions by adding or subtracting them. Adding and subtracting expressions is very similar to adding and subtracting integers and other rational numbers.

Add algebraic expressions by combining like terms.

What is the sum of $(6x^2 + 5x - 3) + (x^2 - 9)$?

Rewrite using the commutative and associative properties to combine like terms.

$$(6x^2 + 5x - 3) + (x^2 - 9) = 6x^2 + x^2 + 5x - 3 - 9$$

Combine like terms. Unlike terms stay the same.

$$6x^2 + x^2 + 5x - 3 - 9 = 7x^2 + 5x - 12$$

The sum of $(6x^2 + 5x - 3) + (x^2 - 9)$ is $7x^2 + 5x - 12$.

Subtract algebraic expressions by adding the opposite of each term in the second expression.

Find the difference.

$$(3p - 5) - (p + 4)$$

Rewrite the expression to add the opposite of each term in the second expression.

$$(3p - 5) + (-p - 4)$$

Combine like terms. Unlike terms stay the same.

$$3p - p - 5 - 4 = 2p - 9$$

The difference of $(3p - 5) - (p + 4)$ is $2p - 9$.

SAMPLE The sum of two expressions is $2n^2 + 5n - 1$. One expression is $3n^2 - 4$. What is the other expression?

A $5n^2 + n - 1$

B $5n^2 + 5n - 5$

C $-n^2 + 5n + 3$

D $-n^2 + 5n - 5$

The correct answer is C. When you know the sum of two expressions and the value of one expression, you subtract to find the value of the other expression. Remember to add the opposite of each term in the second expression of the difference. Then combine like terms:

$$2n^2 + 5n - 1 - (3n^2 - 4) =$$
$$2n^2 + 5n - 1 - 3n^2 + 4 =$$
$$2n^2 - 3n^2 + 5n - 1 + 4 =$$
$$-n^2 + 5n + 3$$

1 Perry wants to simplify the subtraction expression shown below.

$$(2mn - 5m^2) - (4n^2 + 3mn - m^2)$$

Which of the following expressions is equivalent to this subtraction expression?

A $2mn - 5m^2 - 4n^2 + 3mn - m^2$

B $2mn - 5m^2 - 4n^2 - 3mn + m^2$

C $-2mn + 5m^2 - 4n^2 + 3mn - m^2$

D $-2mn + 5m^2 - 4n^2 - 3mn + m^2$

2 What is the sum of the expression below?

$$(8p + q + 5) + (p + q - 7)$$

A $8p + q + 2$

B $8p + q - 2$

C $9p + q - 2$

D $9p + 2q - 2$

3 A quadrilateral is shown below.

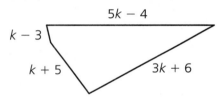

Which expression represents the perimeter of this quadrilateral?

A $10k + 4$

B $10k + 12$

C $12k + 4$

D $12k + 12$

4 Find the sum.

$$(2ab^2 + 6ab - 1) + (a^2b - 3ab - 1)$$

A $3ab^2 - 3ab$

B $3ab^2 - 3ab - 2$

C $2ab^2 + a^2b - 3ab$

D $2ab^2 + a^2b + 3ab - 2$

SAMPLE The perimeter of this triangle is $8x + 4y$.

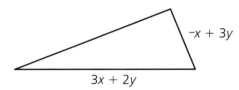

$-x + 3y$

$3x + 2y$

What is the length, in units, of the missing side of this triangle?

Answer _____

 First add the expressions representing the two known side lengths: $(3x + 2y) + (-x + 3y) = 2x + 5y$. Then subtract this sum from the perimeter to find the missing side length: $(8x + 4y) - (2x + 5y) = 8x + 4y - 2x - 5y = 6x - y$. The missing side length is $6x - y$ units.

5 What is the difference of the expression below?

$(-4r + 2s - t) - (2r + s - 5t)$

Answer _____

6 Find the sum.

$(p^4 + 3p^3 - 2p + 1) + (p^3 + 5p^2 - 6p - 4)$

Answer _____

7 Write an expression to show the difference between $12q$ and $4q - r$. Then find the difference.

Answer _____

8 How is subtracting algebraic expressions like subtracting integers?

_____

_____

9 Diane made an error in simplifying the expression shown below.

$$(4xy - 3yz + xz) - (3xy + 3yz - 2xz)$$

Step 1: $4xy - 3yz + xz - 3xy - 3yz + 2xz$

Step 2: $4xy - 3xy - 3yz - 3yz + xz + 2xz$

Step 3: $xy + 3xz$

Part A   Describe Diane's error.

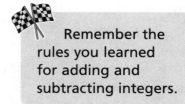

Remember the rules you learned for adding and subtracting integers.

_____

_____

_____

_____

Part B   What is the correct simplified expression? Explain how you found your answer.

_____

_____

_____

Factoring Expressions

7.EE.1

To find the GCF of a set of numbers, first list the factors of each number. Then look for the largest factor common to each number.

Factors
$18 \to$ **1, 2, 3, 6**, 9, 18
$24 \to$ **1, 2, 3**, 4, **6**, 8, 12, 24
$30 \to$ **1, 2, 3**, 5, **6**, 10, 15, 30

Common factors are 1, 2, 3, and 6. The greatest common factor is 6.

Before factoring an algebraic expression, be sure to find the factor common to *all* terms in the expression.

The terms in a fully factored expression have no common factors other than 1.

A **factor** is a number or expression that evenly divides into another with no remainder. To factor an algebraic expression is to find the greatest number or expression that evenly divides each term in the given expression. This is the **greatest common factor (GCF)** of the expression.

What is the GCF of the terms shown below?

$$16x \qquad 20y \qquad 36z$$

None of the variables are the same, so find the GCF of each coefficient.

Factors of 16: 1, 2, 4, 8, 16
Factors of 20: 1, 2, 4, 5, 10, 20
Factors of 36: 1, 2, 3, 4, 6, 9, 12, 18, 36

Common factors of each coefficient are 1, 2, and 4.

4 is the GCF of $16x$, $20y$, and $36z$.

What is the factored form of the expression below?

$$8p^2 - 32pq - 18q^2$$

There are no common variables to all three terms, so first find the GCF of each coefficient in the expression.

Factors of 8:   1, 2, 4, 8
Factors of 32: 1, 2, 4, 8, 16, 32
Factors of 18: 1, 2, 3, 6, 9, 18   The GCF is 2.

Next, divide each term by the GCF.

The factored form is the product of that quotient and the GCF.

$$\frac{8p^2 - 32pq - 18q^2}{2} = 4p^2 - 16pq - 9q^2$$

The factored form of $8p^2 - 32pq - 18q^2$ is $2(4p^2 - 16pq - 9q^2)$.

SAMPLE Which two factors have the product $21n^2 + 7n - 7$?

    A 7 and $3n^2 + n - 1$ **C** 21 and $n^2 + n - 1$

    B 7 and $14n^2 + n - 1$ **D** 21 and $3n^2 + n - 1$

> The correct answer is A. To find two factors, first find the GCF of each term. There are no variables common to all three terms, so find the GCF of 21 and 7. Factors of 21 are 1, 3, 7, and 21. Factors of 7 are 1 and 7. The GCF is 7, so one factor is 7. Divide the expression by 7 to find the other factor: $(21n^2 + 7n - 7) \div 7 = 3n^2 + n - 1$.

1 What is the GCF of $45x^2 + 18y^2$?

    A 6   **C** 18

    B 9   **D** 45

2 Which expression has a GCF of 6?

    A $6w^2 + 8$ **C** $24w^2 + 36$

    B $12w^2 - 3$ **D** $30w^2 - 18$

3 What is the GCF of the expression below?

$$180a + 200ab - 120b$$

    A 10   **C** 30

    B 20   **D** 40

4 What is the factored form of $35y + 21$?

    A $5(7y + 3)$ **C** $7(5y + 3)$

    B $5(7y + 21)$ **D** $7(5y + 21)$

5 The expression $24r + 20s - 36t$ has one factor of 4. What is the other factor?

    A $6r + 5s - 9t$ **C** $6r + 20s - 36t$

    B $8r + 4s - 9t$ **D** $20r + 16s - 32t$

6 The area of a rectangle equals its length times its width. The length of this rectangle is 9 inches.

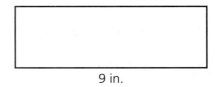

9 in.

The area of the rectangle is $36x - 27y$ square inches. Which expression represents the width, in inches, of this rectangle?

    A $4x - 2y$ **C** $6x - 2y$

    B $4x - 3y$ **D** $6x - 3y$

7 Todd wrote the expression below.

$$12y^4 - 32y^2z^2 + 8z^4$$

Write this expression as the product of two factors.

    A $4(3y^4 - 8y^2z^2 + 2z^4)$

    B $6(2y^4 - 4y^2z^2 + z^4)$

    C $8(2y^4 - 4y^2z^2 + z^4)$

    D $12(y^4 - 32y^2z^2 + 8z^4)$

SAMPLE Ray factored the expression $30x^2 - 90x + 45$ as $5(6x^2 - 18x - 9)$. Is this expression fully factored? Explain how you know.

Answer _____

 No, the expression is not fully factored. If it were, there would be no common factors remaining in the second factor, $6x^2 - 18x - 9$. However, the number 3 is a factor of all of these terms.

8 What is the GCF of the terms shown below?

$$40m^2 \qquad 64mn \qquad 48n$$

Answer _____

9 Factor the expression $27g + 21h + 12j + 18k$.

Answer _____

10 What is the factored form of $20x - 50xy - 25y?$

Answer _____

11 Justine wants to factor the expression $16a - 40b$ by first finding the GCF. How can you tell if she factors out the correct GCF?

_____

_____

12 Collette wants to factor the expression below.

$$80c^3 - 48c + 60$$

Part A What is the GCF of this expression?

Answer _____

Part B What is the factored form of the expression? Show your work.

Answer _____

13 Jacob attempted to fully factor the expression below.

$$8x + 12y - 20z = 2(4x + 6y - 10z)$$

Part A What error did Jacob make factoring this expression?

_____

_____

_____

_____

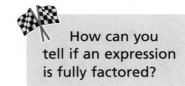

How can you tell if an expression is fully factored?

Part B What is the fully factored form of this expression?

Answer _____

REVIEW

Expressions

Read each problem. Circle the letter of the best answer.

1 Which expression represents twice a number less 5?

   A $2n - 5$ **C** $n + 2 - 5$

   B $5 - 2n$ **D** $5 - n + 2$

2 What are the like terms in the expression below?

$$3hk + 8k + 4h + 6kh$$

   A $8k$ and $4h$

   B $8k$ and $6kh$

   C $3hk$ and $6hk$

   D $3hk$, $8k$, $4h$, and $6kh$

3 What is the GCF of $60a^2 + 36b^2$?

   A 6   **C** 24

   B 12   **D** 36

4 What is the factored form of $96x - 54$?

   A $6(12x - 9)$ **C** $18(5x - 3)$

   B $6(16x - 9)$ **D** $18(6x - 3)$

5 For each question Trent gets correct on a quiz, he earns 5 points. He can also earn an extra 15 bonus points on the quiz. Which expression shows the total possible points Trent can earn on a quiz with q questions?

   A $5q + 15$ **C** $5(q + 15)$

   B $5 + 15q$ **D** $5 + q + 15$

6 What is the difference of the expression below?

$$(12f - 8g + 3h) - (4f - g + 5h)$$

   A $8f - 7g - 2h$ **C** $8f - 9g - 2h$

   B $8f - 7g + 8h$ **D** $8f - 9g + 8h$

7 The perimeter of the quadrilateral below is $9m + 4n - 1$ units.

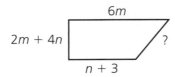

Which expression represents the length, in units, of the missing side?

   A $m - n + 2$ **C** $m + n + 2$

   B $m - n - 4$ **D** $m + n - 4$

8 Winter clothing is on sale for 20% off. Write an expression to represent the total sale cost of a piece of winter clothing that originally costs d.

Answer _____

9 Write this expression in simplest form.

$$6(x - 2y) + 3(2x + y)$$

Answer _____

10 Write an expression to show the difference between $4k + 5$ and $3k^2 - 4$. Then simplify to find the difference.

Answer _____

11 What is the factored form of $20p - 60pq + 32q$?

Answer _____

12 Are the expressions $8a - 3b - (2a - 4b)$ and $6a + b$ equivalent? Explain how you know.

_____

_____

13 Nate factors the expression $30z^3 - 60z^2 - 75z + 25$ as shown below.

$$5(6z^3 - 12z^2 - 25z + 5)$$

Is this expression fully factored? How can you tell?

_____

_____

14 Shelly wrote the expression below.

$$24p^4 - 72p^3 + 16p + 40$$

What is the fully factored form of this expression?

Answer _____

15 Look at this expression.

$$3r^2 - 6r - 2s^2 - 7s + r$$

Part A Which terms are like terms?

Answer _____

Part B What is the simplified form of this expression? Explain how you found your answer.

_____

_____

_____

_____

16 Look at the expression below.

$$27x^2 - 45xy - 18y^2$$

Part A What is the GCF of this expression?

Answer _____

Part B What is the factored form of the expression? Show your work.

Answer _____

Equations and Inequalities

● **Lesson 1 Writing Equations and Inequalities** reviews how to write two-step equations and inequalities to represent problem situations.

● **Lesson 2 Solving Equations** reviews how to solve two-step equations including those representing problem situations.

● **Lesson 3 Solving Inequalities** reviews how to solve two-step inequalities including those representing problem situations and how to graph their solutions on a number line.

Writing Equations and Inequalities

7.EE.4.a, b

Equations use the symbol = to show that two expressions are equal.

An **equation** is a number sentence that shows two expressions are equal. You can use equations to represent real-life situations.

A book club charges a one-time membership fee of $30 and $8 for each book. Jasmine paid $78 for the membership fee and some books. Write an equation that can be used to find the number of books Jasmine bought.

This situation can be represented by the equation below.

cost of the books + membership fee = total paid

The cost of the books equals the price of each book times the number of books. Let b represent the number of books. So, $8b$ represents the cost of the books.

The membership fee is $30 and the total paid is $78.

The equation $8b + 30 = 78$ can be used to find the number of books Jasmine bought.

Inequalities can use any of four symbols:

< "is less than"
> "is greater than"
≤ "is less than or equal to"
≥ "is greater than or equal to"

The symbol ≥ is used to show that *at least* $500 needs to be saved.

The symbol ≤ is used in situations to show *at most* or *no more than.*

An **inequality** is a number sentence that compares two expressions. The symbols $<$, $>$, $\leq$, and $\geq$ are used for comparing. You can use inequalities to represent real-life situations.

Stella wants to buy a $500 bike. So far she has saved $300 and will work to earn the rest. If she earns $8.75 an hour, what is the fewest number of hours Stella needs to work to earn the rest of the money?

This situation can be represented by the inequality below.

amount earned + amount already saved ≥ total amount

The amount earned equals the hourly rate times the number of hours worked. Let h represent the number of hours worked. So, $8.75h$ represents the amount earned.

The amount already saved is $300. The total amount is $500.

The equation $8.75h + 300 \geq 500$ can be used to find the fewest number of hours Stella needs to work.

UNIT 4
Equations and Inequalities

80

SAMPLE Stavros is running in a 5-mile race. So far he has run 2 miles. He wants to know his average running rate for the rest of the race if it takes him $\frac{1}{2}$ hour to finish the rest of the race. Which equation can be used to find r, his average running rate?

A $\frac{1}{2}r + 2 = 5$ C $2(r + \frac{1}{2}) = 5$

B $2r + \frac{1}{2} = 5$ D $\frac{1}{2}(r + 2) = 5$

The correct answer is A. The situation is modeled by this equation: distance already run + distance still to run = total distance. The distance already run is 2 miles. The total distance is 5 miles. The distance still to run is the average running rate times the time to run, or $\frac{1}{2}r$. So the equation used to find r is $2 + \frac{1}{2}r = 5$, or $\frac{1}{2}r + 2 = 5$.

1 A moving company charges $250 to rent a truck and $0.40 for each mile driven. Mr. Lee paid a total of $314. Which equation can be used to find m, the number of miles he drove the moving truck?

A $0.40m + 250 = 314$

B $250m + 0.40 = 314$

C $m + 0.40(250) = 314$

D $m(0.40 + 250) = 314$

2 The width of a rectangle is 6 inches shorter than 3 times its length. The width of the rectangle is at most 45 millimeters. Which inequality can be used to find x, the length of the rectangle?

A $6 - 3x \leq 45$ C $3x - 6 \leq 45$

B $6 - 3x \geq 45$ D $3x - 6 \geq 45$

3 Aiden is 4 inches shorter than twice Jackson's height. Aiden is 68 inches tall. Which equation can be used to find h, Jackson's height in inches?

A $2h - 4 = 68$ C $2(h - 4) = 68$

B $4 - 2h = 68$ D $2(4 - h) = 68$

4 Kristy bought some rolls of wrapping paper and 2 bags of bows for less than $10. Each roll of wrapping paper and each bag of bows cost $1.50. Which inequality can be used to find w, the number of rolls of wrapping paper Kristy bought?

A $1.50w + 2 < 10$

B $2(w + 1.50) < 10$

C $1.50(w + 2) < 10$

D $2(w + 1.50) < 10$

SAMPLE A warehouse elevator can hold at most 1,750 pounds. A 200-pound warehouse worker loads the elevator with boxes that weigh 75 pounds each. The warehouse worker wants to know the maximum number of boxes he can put in the elevator if he is also in the elevator. Write an inequality to describe this situation.

Answer _____

✓ The situation is modeled by this inequality: weight of boxes + weight of worker ≤ the maximum weight. Since the elevator holds at most 1,750 pounds, the symbol ≤ is used. Let b represent the number of boxes. The expression $75b$ represents the weight of the boxes. So the inequality $75b + 200 \leq 1{,}750$ describes this situation.

5 The total cost of a teapot and some teacups is $100. The teapot costs $40. Each teacup costs $10. Write an equation to find t, the total number of teacups bought.

Answer _____

6 Kyle will buy a pair of sunglasses and some bottles of water. He has at most $50 to spend. The sunglasses cost $35. The bottles of water cost $1.40 each. Write an inequality that can be used to find w, the maximum number of bottles of water Kyle can buy.

Answer _____

7 Cheryl and Elaine proofread a 250-page book. Cheryl proofread 20 less than twice as many pages as Elaine proofread. Elaine proofread p pages. Write an equation that can be used to find p.

Answer _____

8 Cory wants to collect at least 150 trading cards. He already has 40 cards. Packs of trading cards contain 12 cards. Write an inequality that can be used to find n, the number of packs of trading cards Cory needs to get.

Answer _____

9 An auto mechanic charges an hourly rate of $74 plus the cost of parts to repair cars.

Part A Write an expression to represent the amount the auto mechanic charges for h hours of repair work.

Answer _____

Part B The cost of parts for one car was $67. The total amount the auto mechanic charged to repair this car was $326. Write an equation to find the number of hours charged to repair this car. Explain how you determined your equation.

_____

_____

_____

10 Nestor has some dimes and $13 worth of quarters.

Part A Write an expression to show the total value of these coins if Nestor has d dimes.

Answer _____

What is the value of 1 dime? 2 dimes? 3 dimes? What expression represents the value of d dimes?

Part B Nestor has more than $15 in quarters and dimes. Write an inequality that can be used to find the number of dimes he has. Explain how you determined your inequality.

_____

_____

_____

Solving Equations

7.EE.4.a

Addition and subtraction are inverse operations.

Multiplication and division are inverse operations.

Equations must be kept in balance. To keep an equation balanced, *always* perform the same operation on *both* sides of the equation.

You can check that an answer is correct by substituting the value of the variable back into the original equation. It should make the equation true.

$x + 6 = 13$ for $x = 7$
$7 + 6 = 13$
$13 = 13$ true

If an equation is in the form $ax + b = c$ or $ax - b = c$, where a, b, and c are rational numbers, undo the addition or subtraction first. Then undo the multiplication or division.

To **solve** an equation means to find the value of the variable that makes the equation true. Inverse operations are used to help solve equations. An **inverse operation** is an operation that "undoes" another operation.

What value of x makes the equation $x + 6 = 13$ true?

This equation uses addition. Use the inverse operation to solve.

The inverse of addition is subtraction. Subtract 6 from both sides of the equation.

$$x + 6 - 6 = 13 - 6$$
$$x = 7$$

The value 7 makes the equation $x + 6 = 13$ true.

Some equations have more than one operation. These require an extra step to solve.

In a game, you can earn 5 points for every gem found, and an extra 50 points for finding all the gems. The equation below shows the total possible points you can earn in the game.

$$5g + 50 = 225$$

What is the value of g, the number of gems in the game?

To solve, first undo the addition by subtracting 50 from both sides.

$$5g + 50 - 50 = 225 - 50$$
$$5g = 175$$

Next, undo the multiplication by dividing 5 into both sides.

$$5g \div 5 = 175 \div 5$$
$$g = 35$$

There are 35 gems in the game.

UNIT 4 ▓▓
Equations and Inequalities

SAMPLE What value of k makes the equation below true?

$$-2(k - 3) = 8$$

A   1   B   -1   C   7   D   -7

The correct answer is B. First use the distributive property to remove the parentheses. Be sure to fully distribute -2 to each term inside the parentheses: $-2k + 6 = 8$. Now, subtract 6 from both sides of the equation: $-2k + 6 - 6 = 8 - 6$, $-2k = 2$. Then divide both sides by -2: $-2k \div -2 = 2 \div -2$, $k = -1$.

1 What value of m makes the equation below true?

$$9m + 36 = 0$$

A   -6   C   4

B   -4   D   6

2 Kyra wants to solve the equation $\frac{x}{10} + 8 = 5$. What steps should she use on both sides of the equation?

A   first divide by 10, then add 8

B   first add 8, then divide by 10

C   first multiply by 10, then subtract 8

D   first subtract 8, then multiply by 10

3 This equation shows the cost, in dollars, of a T-shirt and s pairs of socks.

$$12 + 3s = 42$$

What is the value of s?

A   10   C   16

B   12   D   18

4 A department store sale advertises $\frac{1}{2}$ off all clearance items. Marie buys a clearance item and uses a $5-off coupon. She pays a total of $11. The equation below can be used to find the original price, p, of the clearance item.

$$\frac{1}{2}p - 5 = 11$$

What was the original price of the clearance item?

A $8   C $32

B $12   D $36

5 What value of y makes this equation true?

$$8(y - 9) = 24$$

A   3   C   9

B   6   D   12

6 A tree is 6 feet tall now. It is expected to grow 2 feet a year. In how many years is the tree expected to be 30 feet tall?

A   6   C   16

B   12   D   18

SAMPLE A cell phone company charges $60 for a cell phone and a monthly rate to use the phone. Regina will pay $1,140 for a 24-month cell phone plan. What is the monthly rate for this cell phone plan?

Answer _____

> The equation $24m + 60 = 1,140$ can be used to find the monthly rate, m. To solve this equation, first subtract 60 from both sides: $24m + 60 - 60 = 1,140 - 60$, so $24m = 1,080$. Next, divide both sides by 24 to find m: $24m \div 24 = 1,080 \div 24$, $m = 45$. The monthly rate is $45.

7 Solve this equation for n.

$$-8n - 7 = 31$$

Answer _____

8 The formula $P = 2(L + W)$ can be used to find the perimeter of a rectangle with a length, L, and a width, W. The perimeter of a rectangular shipping crate with a length of 9 feet is 30 feet. What is the width, in feet, of the crate?

Answer _____

9 Describe the steps used to solve the equation below for z. Then find the value of z.

$$3(-2z + 5) = -18$$

_____

_____

_____

_____

UNIT 4
Equations and Inequalities

10 Skylar paid $18 to park at the airport. She bought 4 plane tickets for her family. Each plane ticket cost the same. Altogether, she paid $610 for the plane tickets and parking.

Part A What is the cost for each plane ticket?

Answer _____

Part B Explain how you found your answer.

_____

_____

_____

_____

11 Keith solved the equation $3(t + 7) = 27$ for t using the distributive property to first remove the parentheses.

Part A What value of t makes the equation true?

Answer _____

Part B Hugo solved the same equation by first dividing both sides of the equation by 3, and then subtracting 7 from both sides. Did he use a correct method to solve this equation? Explain how you know.

What value do you get for t by following Hugo's method?

_____

_____

_____

_____

Solving Inequalities

7.EE.4.b

There is only one solution to an equation. There are an **infinite**, or countless, number of solutions to an inequality.

An open dot on a number line means the number is **not** part of the solution. Open dots are used for inequalities with $<$ and $>$.

A closed dot means the number **is** part of the solution. Closed dots are used for inequalities with $\le$ or $\ge$.

The direction of the inequality symbol changes **only** when multiplying or dividing by a negative number.

Change direction:

$-2n < -8 \rightarrow n > 4$

$-\frac{n}{3} \ge 3 \rightarrow n \le -9$

Don't change direction:

$5n \ge -15 \rightarrow n \ge -3$

$n + 3 > 9 \rightarrow n > 6$

$n - 1 \le -6 \rightarrow n \le -5$

To solve an inequality means to find all the values of the variable that make the inequality true. You can use the same steps to solve an inequality as you do to solve an equation.

What is the solution to $3x - 4 > 11$?

Add 4 to both sides to undo subtraction: $3x - 4 + 4 > 11 + 4$
$$3x > 15$$

Divide both sides by 3 to undo multiplication: $3x \div 3 > 15 \div 3$
$$x > 5$$

The solution is all numbers greater than 5.

Solutions to inequalities can be graphed on a number line.

Graph the solution $x > 5$ on a number line.

Draw and label a number line with numbers above and below 5.

Place an open dot at the number in the solution, 5. Draw an arrow from the dot to the right to show the solution includes numbers greater than 5.

When you multiply or divide by a negative number, you must change the direction of the inequality symbol.

What is the solution to $-5x + 6 \le 16$?

Subtract 6 from both sides: $-5x + 6 - 6 \le 16 - 6$
$$-5x \le 10$$

Divide both sides by -5: $-5x \div -5 \le 10 \div -5$
Change the direction of the inequality: $x \ge -2$

The solution is all numbers greater than or equal to -2.

UNIT 4 ▨▨▨▨▨▨▨▨▨▨▨▨▨▨▨▨▨▨▨▨▨▨▨▨▨▨▨▨▨▨▨▨▨▨
Equations and Inequalities

SAMPLE What is the solution to $-\frac{3}{5}x + 4 > 1$?

     A $x > -5$ **B** $x < -5$ **C** $x > 5$ **D** $x < 5$

> The correct answer is D. First subtract 4 from both sides. This gives $-\frac{3}{5}x > -3$. Then multiply both sides by $-\frac{5}{3}$, the reciprocal of $-\frac{3}{5}$. Since you are multiplying by a negative number, change the direction of the inequality symbol from $>$ to $<$. This gives $x < -\frac{3}{1} \cdot -\frac{5}{3}$ or $x < 5$.

1 What is the solution to this inequality?

$$x + 6 \leq 2$$

   A $x \leq -4$ **C** $x \leq 4$

   B $x \geq -4$ **D** $x \geq 4$

2 Which number line shows the solution to the inequality $8x < -8$?

A

B

C

D

3 Gloria set aside $100 to buy school lunches for the year. Each school lunch costs $2. The inequality $100 - 2x < 20$ can be used to find the number of school lunches Gloria can buy before she has less than $20 left. What is the solution to this inequality?

   A $x > 40$ **C** $x > 60$

   B $x < 40$ **D** $x < 60$

4 Which inequality represents the solution to $\frac{2}{3}x + 4 \leq -8$?

   A $x \leq -6$ **C** $x \leq -18$

   B $x \geq -6$ **D** $x \geq -18$

5 Last weekend, seventh graders washed cars for $5 each. They made at least $200. Which inequality represents the number of cars the seventh graders washed?

   A $x \leq 40$ **C** $x \leq 50$

   B $x \geq 40$ **D** $x \geq 50$

6 Which number line shows the solution to the inequality $-2x - 7 \geq -3$?

A

B
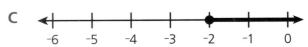

C

D
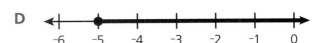

SAMPLE Carter wants to get a grade of at least 85 on his next math test. He loses 3 points for every question he answers incorrectly. The inequality $-3q + 100 \geq 85$ can be used to find the number of questions Carter can answer incorrectly to still get the grade he wants. What is the solution to this inequality?

Answer _____

To solve this inequality, first subtract 100 from both sides. This gives $-3q \geq -15$. Then divide both sides by -3. Be sure to change the direction of the inequality symbol since you are dividing by a negative number. This gives $q \leq 5$.

7 What is the solution to the inequality $\frac{b}{4} - 5 \leq 2$?

Answer _____

8 Graph the solution to the inequality $-p - 4 \geq -7$ on the number line below.

9 Gavin has $20 to spend at an arcade. He spends $8.75 on lunch and plans to use the rest of his money on game tickets. Each game ticket costs $1.25. The inequality $1.25t + 8.75 \leq 20$ can be used to find t, the number of game tickets Gavin can buy. What is the solution to this inequality?

Answer _____

10 Travis has a goal to recycle at least $25 worth of aluminum cans this summer.

- He gets $0.05 for every can he recycles.

- So far he has recycled $8 worth of cans.

Part A Write an inequality to represent the number of additional cans, c, Travis needs to collect in order to reach his goal.

Answer _____

Part B What is the solution to the inequality you wrote in part A? Explain how you found your answer.

_____

_____

_____

_____

11 Haley wrote this inequality.

$$-6x + 3 < -12$$

Part A What values of x make this inequality true? Write your answer as an inequality and graph the solution on this number line.

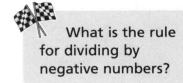

What is the rule for dividing by negative numbers?

Part B Explain how you found your answer.

_____

_____

_____

_____

REVIEW

Equations and Inequalities

Read each problem. Circle the letter of the best answer.

1 A 20-ounce box is filled with cans. Each can weighs 16 ounces. The total weight of the box with cans is 212 ounces. Which equation can be used to find c, the number of cans in the box?

A $16c + 20 = 212$

B $20c + 16 = 212$

C $16(c + 20) = 212$

D $20(c + 16) = 212$

2 Which number line shows the solution to the inequality $4x + 3 > 9$?

A

B

C

D

3 Which inequality represents the solution to $-0.25x + 2.5 \geq 1.5$?

A $x \geq -4$ C $x \geq 0.25$

B $x \leq -0.25$ D $x \leq 4$

4 The second floor in a warehouse is 6 feet higher than $\frac{2}{5}$ the height of the first floor. The height of the second floor is 12 feet. The equation $\frac{2}{5}h + 6 = 12$ can be used to find, h, the height of the first floor. What is the height of the first floor?

A 8 feet   C 24 feet

B 15 feet   D 45 feet

5 Dolores bought 4 books and 4 music CDs at her school fair. Altogether, she spent less than $30. Each book cost $3.50. Each music CD cost the same amount. Which inequality can be used to find m, the cost of each music CD?

A $4m + 3.50 < 30$

B $3.50m + 4 < 30$

C $3.50(m + 4) < 30$

D $4(m + 3.50) < 30$

6 What value of q makes this equation true?

$$-2(q + 8) = -4$$

A -6 C 2

B -2 D 6

7 Fiona spent $13.70 to travel across the city in a taxi. It cost her $3.25 to get the taxi and $2.75 each mile she traveled. Write an equation to find *m*, the total number of miles Fiona traveled.

Answer _____

8 Five more than the product of a number *n* and 8 is at least 100. Write an inequality that can be used to find all possible values of *n*.

Answer _____

9 Solve this equation for *y*.

$$-\frac{1}{2}y - 3 = 7$$

Answer _____

10 Graph the solution to the inequality $-2r + 3 \geq 15$ on the number line below.

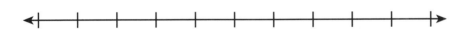

11 Describe the steps used to solve the equation below for *d*. Then find the value of *d*.

$$5(d - 5) = 75$$

_____

_____

_____

12 Eduardo has at most $20 to spend on a canoe rental. To rent a canoe costs $12. To use the canoe costs $3 an hour. Write an inequality that can be used to find *h*, the number of hours Eduardo can use the rented canoe.

Answer _____

13 Vicky bought a basket for $16 and 10 scented soaps to put inside it. Altogether, she paid $51 for the basket and soaps.

Part A What was the cost of each scented soap?

Answer _____

Part B Explain how you found your answer.

_____

_____

_____

_____

14 A company has a budget of no more than $1,000 to advertise a new product. They plan to put an ad in a magazine and to create pamphlets describing the product.

- The magazine ad costs $400.

- The cost for each pamphlet is $2.50.

Part A Write an inequality to represent the possible number of pamphlets, p, the company can create with their budget.

Answer _____

Part B What is the solution to the inequality you wrote in part A? Explain how you found your answer.

_____

_____

_____

_____

Geometry

- **Lesson 1 Scale Drawings** reviews what scale drawings are and how to use them to solve problems.

- **Lesson 2 Constructing Geometric Figures** reviews how to draw geometric figures with a ruler and protractor when given specific information about the figure.

- **Lesson 3 Cross Sections** reviews different types of plane figures and solid figures and how to identify cross sections of solid figures.

- **Lesson 4 Angle Relationships** reviews different types of angle measures and how to use them to find missing angle measures inside geometric figures.

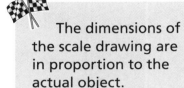

Scale Drawings

7.G.1

The dimensions of the scale drawing are in proportion to the actual object.

Scales can be written just like any ratio: as a fraction, with a colon, or with the word *to.*

$\frac{1}{15}$, 1 : 15, *or* 1 to 15

Be sure to measure with the proper units when using a ruler. If the scale is in centimeters, all ruler measurements should be in centimeters. If the scale is in inches, all ruler measurements should be in inches.

In a proportion, the same units should appear in both numerators and the same units should appear in both denominators.

A **scale drawing** is a diagram, model, or drawing that is larger or smaller than the actual object it represents. The **scale** of a drawing is the ratio that compares the length of the drawing to the actual object.

A model boat is 8 inches long. The actual boat the model represents is 120 feet long. What is the scale of the model?

Write a ratio: $\dfrac{\text{model length}}{\text{actual length}} = \dfrac{8 \text{ inches}}{120 \text{ feet}}$

Simplify the ratio: $\dfrac{8 \text{ inches}}{120 \text{ feet}} = \dfrac{1 \text{ inch}}{15 \text{ feet}}$

The scale is 1 inch : 15 feet.

Rulers, along with ratios and proportions, can be used to solve problems involving scale drawings.

A scale drawing of Renee's bedroom is below. What are the actual dimensions of Renee's bedroom?

Measure the length and width of the drawing with a ruler. The length is 2.5 inches. The width is 2 inches.

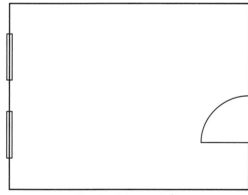

Scale: 1 in. = 5 ft

Set up proportions using the scale to find the actual dimensions.

$$\frac{1 \text{ in.}}{5 \text{ ft}} = \frac{2.5 \text{ in.}}{L \text{ ft}} \qquad\qquad \frac{1 \text{ in.}}{5 \text{ ft}} = \frac{2 \text{ in.}}{W \text{ ft}}$$

$$L = 5 \times 2.5 = 12.5 \text{ ft} \qquad W = 5 \times 2 = 10 \text{ ft}$$

The length of the bedroom is 12.5 feet. The width is 10 feet.

Read each problem. Circle the letter of the best answer.

SAMPLE Part of a map of Northford is shown at the right.

What is the actual distance from the library to the grocery store?

A 1.5 miles   C 6 miles

B 3 miles   D 12 miles

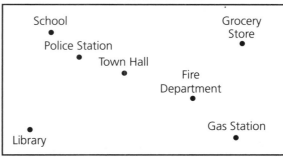

MAP OF NORTHFORD

School

Grocery Store

Police Station

Town Hall

Fire Department

Library

Gas Station

Scale: 2 cm = 0.5 mi

 The correct answer is A. Use a centimeter ruler to measure the distance between the library and the grocery store. This distance is 6 centimeters. Set up and solve a proportion using the given scale: $\frac{2 \text{ cm}}{0.5 \text{ mi}} = \frac{6 \text{ cm}}{x}$, $2x = 3$, so $x = 1.5$ miles.

1 The widest distance across a scale model of the planet Venus is 15 centimeters. The actual widest distance across Venus is approximately 12,000 kilometers. What is the scale of the model of Venus?

A 1 cm to 80 km

B 1 cm to 125 km

C 1 cm to 800 km

D 1 cm to 1,250 km

2 Amber plans to build a scale model of the Washington Monument. She will use a scale of $\frac{1}{200}$ for her model. The actual height of the monument is 555 feet. What should be the height of Amber's scale model?

A 2.25 feet   C 2.775 feet

B 2.50 feet   D 2.875 feet

3 How many years does 1 inch represent on this time line?

0 A.D.   500 A.D.   1,000 A.D.   1,500 A.D.

A 500   C 1,000

B 750   D 1,500

4 A scale drawing of a new ball field is shown below.

Scale: $\frac{1}{2}$ in. = 30 yd

What are the actual dimensions of the ball field?

A 15 yd by 30 yd   C 60 yd by 120 yd

B 30 yd by 60 yd   D 90 yd by 180 yd

SAMPLE A scale model of an ant is shown below.

The actual length of the ant is 0.75 centimeter. What is the scale of this model?

Answer _____

To find the scale, first measure the length of the ant with a centimeter ruler. The length is 9 centimeters. Then write a ratio with the measured length in the numerator and the actual length in the denominator: $\frac{9 \text{ cm}}{0.75 \text{ cm}}$. This ratio can be simplified to $\frac{12 \text{ cm}}{1 \text{ cm}}$.

5 The blueprint at the right represents a scale drawing of an apartment.

Which room has dimensions of 15 feet by 18 feet? Explain how you know.

_____
_____
_____
_____
_____
_____
_____

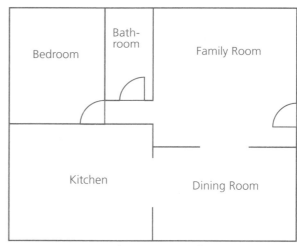

Scale: 1 in. = 12 ft

6 A scale drawing of Colorado is shown below.

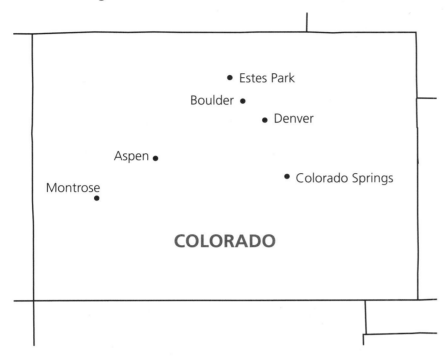

The actual distance across the state of Colorado is 380 miles.

Part A Use your inch ruler to find the scale of this map.

Answer _____

Part B What is the approximate actual distance between Montrose and Colorado Springs? Explain how you know.

_____

_____

_____

_____

_____

Set up a proportion using the scale you found in part A to find the distance.

A **protractor** is a tool used for measuring the size of an angle.

The angle measures in a triangle sum to 180°. The angle measures in a **quadrilateral,** or 4-sided figure, sum to 360°.

A protractor has two rows of angle measures. One reads from left to right. The other reads from right to left. Be sure you measure and mark angles based on the correct row.

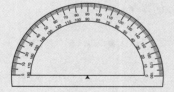

Sometimes more than one triangle can be drawn with given measurements. Other times, it is not possible to draw a triangle with given measurements.

You can use a ruler and a protractor to construct geometric figures.

Two sides of a triangle are 6 centimeters and 4 centimeters long. The angle between those two sides measures 50°. Use a ruler and a protractor to draw this triangle.

With the straightedge of the ruler, draw a line segment 6 centimeters long.

6 cm

Line up the bottom of the protractor with the line segment. Put the center of the protractor at one end of the segment. Mark the point on the protractor measuring 50°. Draw another line segment connecting the point to the end of the first segment.

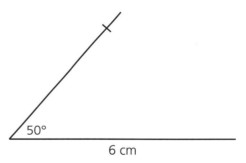

Measure a length of 4 centimeters on the line you just drew. Start from the point where the 50° angle forms. Mark this point and connect it to the other end of the 6-centimeter segment to form a triangle.

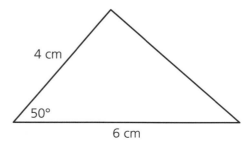

SAMPLE A triangle has angles that measure 40° and 75°. The length of the side between these angles is 5 centimeters. Which measures are closest to the lengths of the other two sides of this triangle?

    A 3 cm and 4 cm   **C** 4 cm and 6 cm

    B 3.5 cm and 5.5 cm   **D** 4.5 cm and 6.5 cm

The correct answer is B. Draw a segment 5 cm long. From one end, draw a 40° angle. From the other end, draw a 75° angle. Connect the sides to form a triangle. With a ruler, measure the two sides you just drew. They measure about 3.5 cm and 5.5 cm.

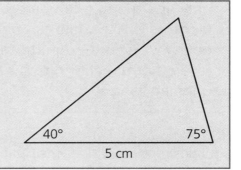

1 Which figure is **not** possible to draw?

    A A triangle with three 3-in. sides.

    B A quadrilateral with four 3-in. sides.

    C A triangle with exactly two 90° angles.

    D A quadrilateral with exactly two 90° angles.

2 A triangle has angle measures of 80° and 45°. How many possible triangles can be drawn with these measures?

    A 0   **C** 2

    B exactly 1   **D** more than 2

3 A triangle has side lengths of 1.5 inches and 3 inches. One angle measures 100°. How many possible triangles can be drawn with these measurements?

    A 0   **C** 2

    B exactly 1   **D** more than 2

4 A quadrilateral has side lengths that are all 8 cm long. One angle measures 65°. Which statement must be true?

    A It is not possible to draw this quadrilateral.

    B It is possible to draw more than one quadrilateral with these measures.

    C The other angles in this quadrilateral measure 115°, 65°, and 115°.

    D The other angles in this quadrilateral measure 115°, 90°, and 90°.

5 A triangle has two side lengths of 2 inches and 5 inches. The angle between these sides measures 70°. What are the approximate measures of the other two angles in this triangle?

    A 25° and 85°   **C** 35° and 75°

    B 30° and 80°   **D** 40° and 70°

SAMPLE How many unique triangles can be drawn with side lengths of 2.5 inches, 2.5 inches, and 2 inches?

Answer _____

When three sides of a triangle are known, only one triangle can be drawn with the lengths. This triangle can only be formed one way. Even though it can be turned to face other directions, this is still one unique triangle.

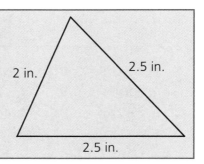

6 Draw a triangle with two sides measuring 5 centimeters each and the angle between them measuring 130°. Label the given sides and angle.

7 How many different triangles can be drawn with side lengths of 3 inches and 4 inches, and an angle measuring 90°—no triangle, one triangle, or more than one triangle? Explain how you know.

_____

_____

8 A triangle has a base of 1.5 inches. The angles at each end of this base measure 50° and 90°. Draw this triangle in the space at the right. Label the lengths of the sides and the measures of the angles.

9 Cyril drew a quadrilateral with exactly two sides that measure 2 inches each and exactly one angle that measures 90°.

Part A In the space below, draw a quadrilateral with these measurements.

Part B Warren wants to draw a different quadrilateral with these same measurements. Explain two possible ways he can do this.

How can the given measurements be moved around to still form a quadrilateral?

_____

_____

_____

_____

Cross Sections

7.G.3

A **plane figure** is a flat, two-dimensional shape such as a square, triangle, rectangle, or circle. A **solid figure** is a three-dimensional shape that takes up space. Examples of solid figures are prisms, pyramids, cylinders, and cones.

Rectangular Prism

Rectangular Pyramid

Cylinder

Cone

A **cross section** of a solid figure is the resulting plane figure you get when you slice through the solid object.

The rectangular prism below has square bases.

Which plane figures represent the horizontal and vertical cross sections of this prism?

For the horizontal cross section, imagine a plane slicing the rectangular prism from left to right. The resulting cross section matches the top and bottom of the prism, which are squares.

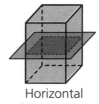
Horizontal Cross section

For the vertical cross section, imagine a plane slicing the rectangular prism from top to bottom. The resulting cross section matches the sides of the prism, which are rectangles.

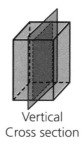
Vertical Cross section

The sides of a prism are always rectangles. The sides of a pyramid are always triangles.

A horizontal cross section is parallel to the top and bottom of a solid. A vertical cross section is parallel to the sides of a solid.

Some cross sections are formed by slanted planes. These cross sections may not look like any face, or side, on the geometric shape.

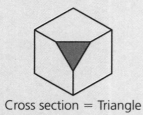
Cross section = Triangle

UNIT 5
Geometry

SAMPLE Which of the following shapes represents the vertical cross section of this cylinder?

A   circle   C   triangle

B   square   D   rectangle

 The correct answer is D. A vertical cross section slices through the top and bottom of a solid figure. The resulting plane figure is a rectangle.

1 Which shape has a triangular vertical cross section?

A   C

B   D

2 Which shape represents the horizontal cross section of this square pyramid?

A   C

B   D

3 Which solid figure has the horizontal and vertical cross sections shown below?

Horizontal   Vertical
Cross section   Cross section

A   cone

B   cylinder

C   rectangular prism

D   rectangular pyramid

4 A cube is shown below.

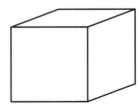

Which of the following plane figures is **not** a possible cross section of the cube?

A   square   C   circle

B   rectangle   D   triangle

SAMPLE A triangular prism is shown at the right.

What plane figures make up the horizontal and vertical cross sections of this triangular prism?

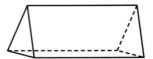

Horizontal _____

Vertical _____

   A horizontal cross section slices the solid from left to right. This cross section is parallel to the bottom of the prism, which is a rectangle. A vertical cross section slices the solid from top to bottom. This cross section is parallel to the sides of the prism, which are triangles.

5 A rectangular pyramid is shown below.

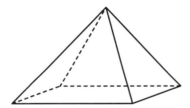

Draw and label the plane figures that form the horizontal and vertical cross sections of this pyramid.

6 Name a solid figure that has the same plane figure as a horizontal cross section and a vertical cross section. Explain how you know.

_____

_____

_____

7 Morgan and Hector have different solid figures. Morgan has the solid shown below.

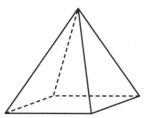

Part A What two plane figures are formed by the horizontal and vertical cross sections of Morgan's solid figure?

Imagine the solid figure being sliced in half from left to right, and from top to bottom.

Horizontal _____

Vertical _____

Part B The horizontal and vertical cross sections of Hector's solid figure are shown below.

What type of solid figure does Hector have? Explain how you know.

_____

_____

_____

_____

Angle Relationships

7.G.5

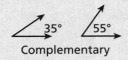
35° 55°
Complementary

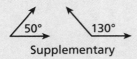
50° 130°
Supplementary

Two complementary angles put together form a right angle.

35°
55°

Two supplementary angles put together form a straight line.

50° 130°

The symbol m∠A means "the measure of angle A."

Congruent angles have the same measure, so all vertical angles have the same measure.

Two angles are **complementary** if the sum of their measures equals 90°. Two angles are **supplementary** if the sum of their measures equals 180°.

In the diagram at the right, $\overleftrightarrow{FH}$ is a straight line and m∠FGJ is 90°.

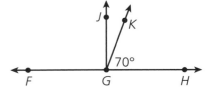

What is m∠JGK?

Since $\overleftrightarrow{FH}$ is a straight line, ∠FGJ and ∠JGH are supplementary. So, m∠FGJ + m∠JGH = 180°.

$$m\angle JGH = 180° - m\angle FGJ = 180° - 90° = 90°$$

This means m∠JGK + m∠KGH = 90°.

$$m\angle JGK = 90° - m\angle KGH = 90° - 70° = 20°$$

The measure of ∠JGK is 20°.

Angles are formed by lines that intersect. Opposite angles formed by intersecting lines are **vertical** angles. All pairs of vertical angles are congruent. **Adjacent** angles are angles that are next to each other.

Lines *j* and *k* intersect and m∠1 = 45°.

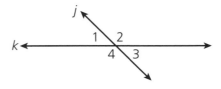

What are the measures of ∠2, ∠3, and ∠4?

Angles 1 and 3 are vertical, so m∠1 = m∠3 = 45°.

Angles 1 and 2 are supplementary, so m∠1 + m∠2 = 180°.

$$m\angle 2 = 180° - 45° = 135°$$

Angles 2 and 4 are vertical, so m∠2 = m∠4 = 135°.

SAMPLE Which pair of angles must be congruent in the diagram at the right?

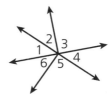

A ∠1 and ∠2   C ∠3 and ∠6

B ∠1 and ∠4   D ∠5 and ∠6

   The correct answer is B. Vertical angles are always congruent. Angles 1 and 2 and angles 5 and 6 are adjacent, so they may not be congruent. It looks like angles 3 and 6 are vertical, but they are not formed by a pair of intersecting straight lines. The only angles that are vertical are angles 1 and 4.

1 Which pair of angles are adjacent?

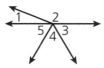

A ∠1 and ∠3   C ∠2 and ∠4

B ∠2 and ∠3   D ∠3 and ∠5

2 In the diagram below, lines *l* and *m* intersect.

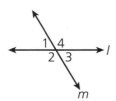

The measure of ∠4 is 133°. Which equation can be used to find m∠3?

A m∠3 + 90° = 133°

B m∠3 − 90° = 133°

C m∠3 + 133° = 180°

D m∠3 − 133° = 180°

3 Angles *P* and *Q* are supplementary and m∠P = 30°. What is m∠Q?

A 60°   C 120°

B 70°   D 150°

4 Angles *R* and *S* are congruent and form a right angle. What is m∠S?

A 45°   C 90°

B 50°   D 100°

5 In the diagram below, m∠2 = 90°.

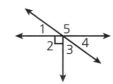

Which statement must be true?

A ∠2 and ∠5 are vertical.

B ∠3 and ∠4 are congruent.

C ∠1 and ∠3 are complementary.

D ∠2, ∠3, and ∠4 are supplementary.

SAMPLE Right triangle *PQR* is shown at the right.

What is the measure of the angle marked *z?*

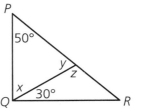

Answer _____

 Angle *Q* is a right angle, so it measures 90°. So, $x + 30° = 90°$ and $x = 60°$. The sum of the angles in any triangle is 180°. So, $x + y + 50° = 180°$ and $y = 180° - 50° - 60° = 70°$. Angles *y* and *z* are supplementary, so $70° + z = 180°$ and $z = 110°$.

6 In the diagram below, $m\angle 1 = 75°$.

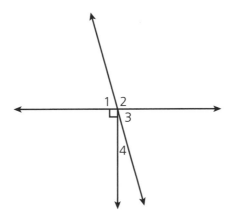

What are the measures of ∠2, ∠3, and ∠4?

m∠2 _____   m∠3 _____   m∠4 _____

7 Eric thinks the angles in any triangle are supplementary. Is he correct?
Explain how you know.

_____

_____

_____

8 In the diagram below, ∠3 is complementary to ∠4. The measure of ∠3 is 35°.

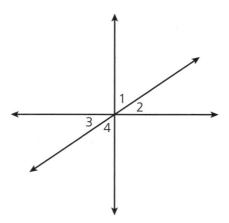

Part A Write an equation that can be used to find the measure of ∠4.

Answer _____

Part B In the diagram above, ∠1 is vertical to ∠4. What is the measure of ∠1? Explain how you know.

_____

_____

9 Angle *X* is complementary to angle *Y*. Angle *X* is supplementary to angle *Z*. The measure of angle *Z* is 102°.

Part A What is the measure of angle *Y*?

Answer _____

Part B Explain how you found your answer to part A.

What equations can you write to show the relationship between angles *X*, *Y*, and *Z*?

_____

_____

_____

_____

REVIEW

Geometry

Read each problem. Circle the letter of the best answer.

1 A triangle has two angle measures of 50° each and a side between these angles measuring 0.5 meter. How many possible triangles can be drawn with these measures?

A 0   **C** 2

B exactly 1   **D** more than 2

2 Which shape represents the vertical cross section of this prism?

A   **C**

B   **D**

3 Angles R and S are complementary. The measure of $\angle R$ is 31°. Which equation can be used to find $m\angle S$?

A $31° + m\angle S = 90°$

B $m\angle S - 31° = 90°$

C $31° + m\angle S = 180°$

D $m\angle S - 31° = 180°$

4 The map below shows some towns in Oakland County.

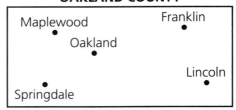

OAKLAND COUNTY

The actual distance between Springdale and Franklin is 30 miles. Which scale is most appropriate for this map?

A 1 cm = 5 mi   **C** 1 cm = 6 mi

B 1 cm = 5.5 mi   **D** 1 cm = 7.5 mi

5 Which solid figure has the horizontal and vertical cross sections shown below?

Horizontal Cross section   Vertical Cross section

A cone   **C** cylinder

B prism   **D** pyramid

6 A triangle has side lengths that are 3.5 inches and 4.75 inches. The angle between these sides measures 60°. What is the length of the third side?

Answer _____

7 A scale drawing of a bookcase is shown here.

What are the actual dimensions of the bookcase?

Answer _____

Scale: $\frac{1}{4}$ in. = 1 ft

8 Draw and label a triangle with two angles measuring 35° and 105° and the side between them measuring 2.5 inches.

9 A right triangle is shown in the diagram below.

What is m∠1?

Answer _____

10 In the diagram below, m∠1 = 74°.

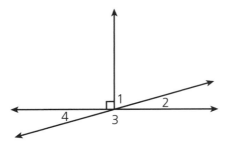

Part A What is m∠2?

Answer _____

Part B What is m∠3? Explain how you know.

_____

_____

11 On △LMN, LM = 7 centimeters and MN = 5 centimeters. One of the angles in △LMN measures 108°.

Part A Which of the angles in △LMN must be 108°?

Answer _____

Part B Explain how you know your answer to part A is correct.

_____

_____

_____

_____

UNIT 6

Area and Volume

● **Lesson 1 Circumference and Area** reviews how to find the area and circumference of a circle and how to use these measures to solve problems.

● **Lesson 2 Area** reviews how to find the area of triangles, quadrilaterals, and other polygons and how to use area to solve problems.

● **Lesson 3 Surface Area** reviews how to find the surface area of prisms and objects made from prisms and how to use surface area to solve problems.

● **Lesson 4 Volume** reviews how to find the volume of prisms and objects made from prisms and how to use volume to solve problems.

Circumference and Area

7.G.4

Pi is a number with a value of 3.1415926…. An approximate value of pi is 3.14.

The symbol for pi is π.

The distance around a circle is called the **circumference.** To find the circumference, multiply the **diameter, d,** or longest distance across a circle, by pi. The formula for circumference is $C = \pi d$.

The diameter of this clock is 50 centimeters.

What is the approximate circumference of the clock?

Use the formula for circumference. The diameter is 50 centimeters. Use 3.14 for π.

$$C = \pi d$$
$$C = 3.14(50) = 157$$

The circumference of the clock is approximately 157 cm.

Circumference is measured in linear units such as inches (in.), feet (ft), and meters (m).

The radius of a circle always equals half the diameter.

$$r = \frac{1}{2}d \ \text{ or } \ d = 2r$$

Read r^2 as "radius squared." To square a number, multiply the number by itself.

$$5^2 = 5 \times 5 = 25$$

Area is measured in square units such as square inches (in.^{2}), square feet (ft^2), and square meters (m^2).

Area is the space inside a figure. To find the area of a circle, multiply pi by the square of the radius. The **radius, r,** is the distance from the center of a circle to its edge. The formula for area of a circle is $A = \pi r^2$.

What is the approximate area inside the clock shown above?

Use the formula for area of a circle. The diameter is 50 centimeters, so the radius is 25 centimeters. Use 3.14 for π.

$$A = \pi r^2$$
$$A = 3.14(25)^2 = 3.14(625) = 1{,}962.5$$

The area of the clock is approximately 1,962.5 cm^2.

SAMPLE The radius of a circle is 10 centimeters. What is the circumference of the circle?

    A   5π cm   **B**   10π cm   **C**   20π cm   **D**   25π cm

> **The correct answer is C. The formula for the circumference of a circle is C = πd. Since the diameter equals twice the radius, d = 2(10) = 20 centimeters. So, the circumference of the circle is 20π centimeters.**

1 The diameter of a circle is 3 meters. What is the radius of this circle?

    A   1.5 meters   **C**   6 meters

    B   3 meters   **D**   9 meters

2 The diagram below represents a ride at a carnival.

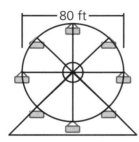

This ride moves along in a circular path. What is the approximate distance, in feet, of one complete loop of this path?

    A   83.14 feet   **C**   240.14 feet

    B   125.6 feet   **D**   251.2 feet

3 The radius of the circular lens of a magnifying glass is 4 centimeters. What is the area, in square centimeters, of the glass?

    A   4π cm²   **C**   16π cm²

    B   8π cm²   **D**   64π cm²

4 The radius of a circular rug is 30 inches. What is the approximate circumference, in inches, of this rug?

    A   47.1 inches   **C**   188.4 inches

    B   94.2 inches   **D**   282.6 inches

5 The plastic lid for a food storage container is shown below.

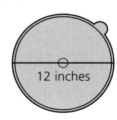

12 inches

What is the approximate area, in square inches, of the lid?

    A   18.84 in.²   **C**   75.36 in.²

    B   37.68 in.²   **D**   113.04 in.²

6 A circular dance stage has a perimeter of 28π feet. What is the area, in square feet, of this dance stage?

    A   56π ft²   **C**   280π ft²

    B   196π ft²   **D**   784π ft²

SAMPLE This basketball hoop has a circular rim. The circumference of the rim is 56.52 inches.

What is the length of the diameter of the hoop? Use 3.14 for π.

Answer _____

 To find the diameter, use the circumference formula with the given values: $C = \pi d$, so $56.52 = 3.14d$. Now divide both sides by 3.14: $56.52 \div 3.14 = 3.14d \div 3.14$, so $d = 18$ inches.

7 The radius of a circular plate is 12 centimeters. What is the area, in square centimeters, of this plate? Write your answer using π.

Answer _____

8 A pizza has a 14-inch diameter. What is the approximate area, in square inches, of the pizza? Use 3.14 for π.

Answer _____

9 The circumference of this circle is approximately 31.4 meters.

What is the length, in meters, of the radius of this circle? Use 3.14 for π.

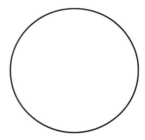

Answer _____

10 A circle has a diameter of 6 inches. Hoshi found the area by wrongly using the diameter instead of the radius in the area formula. How many times greater is the area of the circle Hoshi found compared to the actual area? Explain how you know.

_____

_____

_____

11 A circular mirror has a diameter of 16 inches.

Part A What is the area, in square inches, of this mirror? Write your answer using π.

Answer _____

Part B The frame around the mirror is 3 inches wide, as shown here.

What is the circumference, in inches, of the outside of the frame around the mirror? Write your answer using π. Explain how you know.

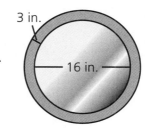

3 in.

16 in.

If the frame is 3 inches wide, by how much does the diameter of the circle increase?

_____

_____

_____

12 A circular stage has a radius of 8 feet. Flynn wants to paint a red line along the edge of the stage. He calculates its approximate circumference this way: 3.14(8)(8) = 3.14(64) = 200.96 square feet.

Part A What error did Flynn make in his calculation?

Answer _____

Part B Flynn also wants to paint the stage floor. One quart of paint covers about 75 square feet of space. What is the fewest quarts of paint Flynn will need? Explain how you know.

_____

_____

_____

Area

7.G.6

A rectangle is a quadrilateral with 4 congruent angles. The formula for the area of a rectangle with length *l* and width *w* is $A = lw$.

A square is a rectangle with 4 congruent sides. The formula for the area of a square with side length *s* is $A = s^2$.

Composite figures are shapes made up of more than one figure.

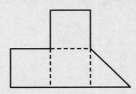

Some polygons have special names based on the number of sides they have.

Pentagon: 5 sides
Hexagon: 6 sides
Octagon: 8 sides
Decagon: 10 sides

Area can be found for any polygon. A **polygon** is a figure with straight sides that connect to each other. A **triangle** is a polygon with 3 sides. A **quadrilateral** is a polygon with 4 sides. The **area formulas** for a triangle and some quadrilaterals are below.

Triangle: $A = \frac{1}{2} \times$ base $\times$ height $= \frac{1}{2}bh$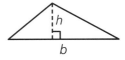

Parallelogram: $A =$ base $\times$ height $= bh$

Trapezoid: $A = \frac{1}{2} \times$ (base₁ + base₂) $\times$ height
$= \frac{1}{2} \times (b_1 + b_2)h$

These area formulas can be used to find the area of polygons and composite figures.

What is the area of this pentagon?

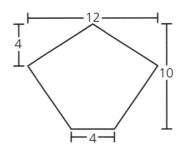

Area of pentagon = area of triangle + area of trapezoid

Area $= \frac{1}{2}bh + \frac{1}{2}(b_1 + b_2)h$

Area $= \frac{1}{2}(12)(4) + \frac{1}{2}(12 + 4)(6)$

Area $= \frac{1}{2}(48) + \frac{1}{2}(96)$

Area $= 24 + 48$

Area $= 72$ square units

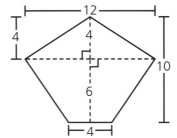

SAMPLE The diagram at right shows the shape of a dance floor.

What is the total area of the dance floor?

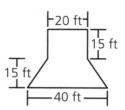

A 550 ft²

C 800 ft²

B 750 ft²

D 900 ft²

 The correct answer is B. The dance floor can be divided into a rectangle and a trapezoid. The area of the rectangle is 20(15) = 300 square feet. The area of the trapezoid is $\frac{1}{2}$(20 + 40)(15) = 450 square feet. The total area is 300 + 450 = 750 square feet.

1 A rectangular welcome mat is 30 inches long and 24 inches wide. What is the area of the welcome mat?

A 54 in.²

C 360 in.²

B 108 in.²

D 720 in.²

2 A triangular sail on a boat has a height of 15 yards and a length of 12 yards. What is the area of the sail?

A 27 yd²

C 90 yd²

B 54 yd²

D 180 yd²

3 What is the area of the figure below?

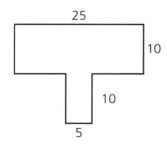

A 50 sq units

C 250 sq units

B 100 sq units

D 300 sq units

4 This hexagon is made up of three congruent parallelograms.

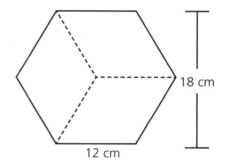

What is the area of the hexagon?

A 324 cm²

C 648 cm²

B 360 cm²

D 2,160 cm²

5 This figure represents the shape of a flower garden.

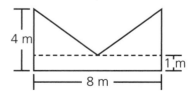

What is the area of the garden?

A 16 m²

C 24 m²

B 20 m²

D 32 m²

SAMPLE Four congruent triangles are cut from a square piece of glass to make the octagonal window shown here.

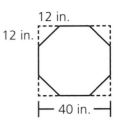
12 in.

12 in.

40 in.

What is the area, in square inches, of the window?

Answer _____

First find the area of the square. Then subtract the areas of each triangle to find the area of the octagon. The area of the square is $40^2 = 1,600$ in.^{2}. The area of one triangle is $\frac{1}{2}(12)(12) = 72$ in.^{2}. The area of the octagon is $1,600 - 4(72) = 1,312$ in.^{2}.

6 A rhombus is a quadrilateral with four congruent sides. What is the area, in square centimeters, of this rhombus?

16 cm   20 cm

Answer _____

7 This figure represents a piece of cardboard. What is the area, in square inches, of the cardboard?

10 in.   50 in.

20 in.

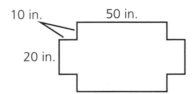

Answer _____

8 Phil found the area of this triangle using the calculation below.

Area $= \frac{1}{2}(18) \cdot \frac{1}{2}(15) = 67\frac{1}{2}$ sq cm

What error did Phil make in his calculation?

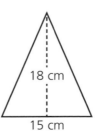
18 cm

15 cm

Answer _____

UNIT 6 ▓▓▓
Area and Volume

9 A square has a side length of 50 millimeters.

Part A What is the area, in square millimeters, of the square?

Answer _____

Part B The figure below is made up of two triangles. Its total area is the same as the square in part A.

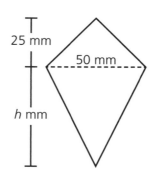

Subtract the area of the top triangle from the total area to help find the height of the bottom triangle.

What is the value of *h,* in millimeters? Explain how you know.

_____

_____

_____

10 Briana cut shape Z from the figure shown here.

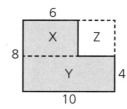

Part A Write an expression for the area of the shaded figure using expressions for shapes X and Y.

Answer _____

Part B Write an expression for the shaded figure using an expression for shape Z. Is this area the same as the area from the expression in part A? Explain why or why not.

_____

_____

Surface Area

7.G.6

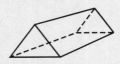

A **prism** is a solid figure with two congruent polygon bases and rectangular sides.

The bases of a prism can be any polygon.

Triangular Prism

Square Prism

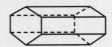

Hexagonal Prism

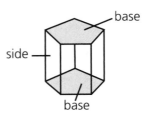

Surface area is always measured in square units.

The formula for the surface area of a cube with side s is $SA = 6s^2$.

The **surface area** of a solid figure is the sum of the areas of all its sides.

Surface area of prism = areas of two bases + areas of sides

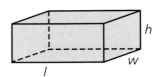

The formula for the surface area of a rectangular prism with length l, width w, and height h is

$$SA = 2lw + 2lh + 2wh$$

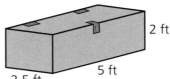

A woodworker charges $2 per square foot for each storage box he builds. What amount would he charge for the storage box below?

2 ft
5 ft
2.5 ft

Use the formula for the surface area of a rectangular prism to find the total surface area.

l = 5 feet, w = 2.5 feet, and h = 2 feet
$$SA = 2lw + 2lh + 2wh$$
$$= 2(5)(2.5) + 2(5)(2) + 2(2.5)(2)$$
$$= 25 + 20 + 10$$
$$= 55 \text{ square feet}$$

Multiply the total surface area by the cost per square foot.

$$\$2 \times 55 = \$110$$

The woodworker would charge $110 for this storage box.

SAMPLE The diagram at the right represents a shed. What is the total surface area of the shed, including its top and its floor?

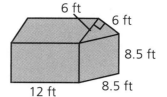

6 ft
6 ft
8.5 ft
8.5 ft
12 ft

A 630.5 ft²   C 867 ft²

B 732.5 ft²   D 1,299 ft²

The correct answer is A. The shed is made up of a triangular prism for the top and a rectangular prism for the bottom. Add the surface areas, minus the faces that meet, for both to find the total surface area. The surface area of the top includes two triangular bases and two rectangular roof sides: $SA = 2\left(\frac{1}{2}(6)(6)\right) + 2(6)(12) = 36 + 144 = 180$ square feet. The surface area of the bottom includes two square bases, two rectangular sides, and one rectangular floor: $SA = 2(8.5)(8.5) + 2(8.5)(12) + (8.5)(12) = 144.5 + 204 + 102 = 450.5$ square feet. The total surface area $= 180 + 450.5 = 630.5$ square feet.

1 A cube has a side length of 15 millimeters. What is the surface area of the cube?

A 90 mm²   C 540 mm²

B 225 mm²   D 1,350 mm²

2 Each side length on the base of this prism measures 5 feet.

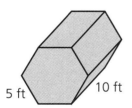

5 ft   10 ft

The area of each base is approximately 52 square feet. What is the approximate total surface area of the prism?

A 202 ft²   C 404 ft²

B 352 ft²   D 520 ft²

3 A shoebox in the shape of a rectangular prism is 10 inches long, 8 inches wide, and 6 inches tall. What is the surface area of the shoebox?

A 188 in.²   C 376 in.²

B 280 in.²   D 480 in.²

4 The three cubes shown below are glued together and will be painted.

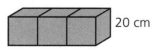

20 cm

What is the total surface area that will be painted?

A 2,800 cm²   C 6,000 cm²

B 5,600 cm²   D 7,200 cm²

SAMPLE Each cube in this stack has a side length 1 unit long.

What is the total surface area, in square units, of the cubes?

Answer _____

 Each side of the cubes has an area of 1 × 1 = 1 square unit. To find the total surface area, count the total number of sides. Some sides are hidden, but need to be counted as well. There are 5 sides on the front, and 5 on the back. There are 3 sides on the top, and 3 on the bottom. There are 2 sides on the left, and 2 on the right. Altogether, there are 5 + 5 + 3 + 3 + 2 + 2 = 20 square units.

5 What is the total surface area, in square meters, of this prism?

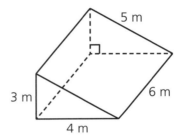

Answer _____

6 Taylor made this jewelry box by combining two rectangular boxes.

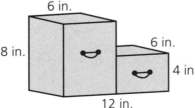

What is the total surface area, in square inches, of this jewelry box?

Answer _____

7 This diagram shows the front and side views of a mailbox that attaches to a house.

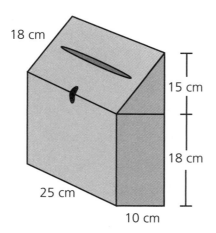

18 cm

15 cm

18 cm

25 cm

10 cm

Part A What two solid figures make up this mailbox?

Answer _____

Part B Donovan plans to paint this mailbox except for its back. What is the total surface area, in square centimeters, that he will paint? Show your work.

> Remember to include the area of hidden sides in your calculation for surface area. Which sides are hidden?

Answer _____

Volume

7.G.6

The area of the base of this octagonal prism is 10 m².

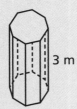

3 m

V = area of base × height

$V = 10 \times 3 = 30$ m³

Volume is always measured in cubic units. For example:

cubic feet = ft³
cubic inches = in.³
cubic meters = m³

The formula for the volume of a cube with side s is $V = s^3$.

Volume is the amount of space inside a solid figure or object.

Volume of prism = area of base × height

The formula for the volume of a rectangular prism with length l, width w, and height h is

Volume = length × width × height

$$V = l \times w \times h$$

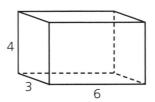

4

3   6

$$V = 6 \times 3 \times 4 = 72 \text{ cubic units}$$

You can use the volume formula to solve problems.

This fish tank holds 3.75 cubic feet of water.

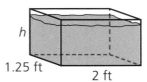

h

1.25 ft   2 ft

What is h, the height of the water in the fish tank?

You know the volume and you know the length and width of the fish tank. Substitute these values into the volume formula to find the height of the water.

$$V = l \times w \times h$$
$$3.75 = 2 \times 1.25 \times h$$
$$3.75 = 2.5 \times h$$
$$3.75 \div 2.5 = 2.5 \div 2.5 \times h$$
$$1.5 = h$$

The height of the water in the fish tank is 1.5 feet.

SAMPLE What is the total volume of the solid figure shown here?

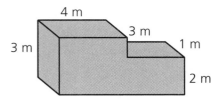

A   13 m³   C   24 m³

B   18 m³   D   36 m³

 The correct answer is B. The solid figure is made up of a small rectangular prism on top of a larger one. Add both volumes to find the total volume. Top prism: l = 4 m, w = 1 m, and h = 3 − 2 = 1 m. So, V = 4 × 1 × 1 = 4 m³. Bottom prism: l = 4 + 3 = 7 m, w = 1 m, and h = 2 m. So, V = 7 × 1 × 2 = 14 m³. The total volume = 4 + 14 = 18 m³.

1 A cube has a side length of 5 centimeters. What is the volume of the cube?

A   15 cm³   C   125 cm³

B   25 cm³   D   150 cm³

2 A cereal box is a rectangular prism. Its length is 10 inches, its width is 3 inches, and its height is 14 inches. What is its volume?

A   170 in.³   C   320 in.³

B   270 in.³   D   420 in.³

3 A tent has the shape of a triangular prism.

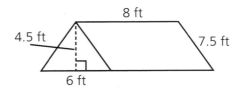

What is the volume inside this tent?

A   101.25 ft³   C   202.5 ft³

B   108 ft³   D   216 ft³

4 The side length of each cube is 3 cm.

What is the total volume of this stack?

A   27 cm³   C   243 cm³

B   108 cm³   D   324 cm³

5 A triangular prism is attached to a cube.

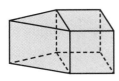

The area of the base of the triangular prism is 25 square inches. The volume of the triangular prism is 100 square inches. What is the volume of the cube?

A   16 in.³   C   64 in.³

B   40 in.³   D   96 in.³

SAMPLE Books of the same size are stacked on top of each other. The dimensions of each book are 11 inches by 6 inches by 1.5 inches. The total volume of the stack of books is 495 cubic inches. How many books are in the stack?

Answer _____

 First find the volume of each book: $V = 11 \times 6 \times 1.5 = 99$ in.^{3}. Divide this into the total volume to find the number of books in the stack: $495 \div 99 = 5$ books.

6 Each base of this pentagonal prism has an area of 40 square yards.

What is the total volume, in cubic yards, of this prism?

Answer _____

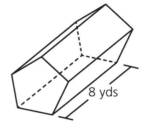
8 yds

7 Cubes with a volume of 1 cubic centimeter each fill a box. There are 4 rows of cubes in the box. Each row is 8 cubes long and 5 cubes wide. What is the total volume inside the box?

Answer _____

8 This diagram shows the dimensions of a playhouse.

What is the total amount of space, in cubic feet, inside the playhouse?

Answer _____

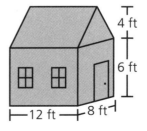
4 ft
6 ft
12 ft   8 ft

9 A baker charges $2.00 per serving for each cake he makes. Each serving is 12 cubic inches.

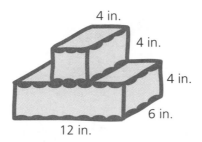

Part A How many servings are in the cake shown? Show your work.

Answer _____

Part B What is the total amount the baker would charge for this cake?

Answer _____

10 The sides of this hexagonal drum are all the same length.

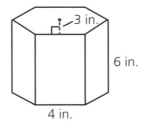

Part A What is the volume, in cubic inches, of the drum?

Answer _____

Part B Explain how you found your answer.

A 216 in³
36 X 6 =
216 in³
2 X 6 + 12

_____
_____
_____
_____

REVIEW

Area and Volume

Read each problem. Circle the letter of the best answer.

1 This sign has a height of 16 inches and a base length of 20 inches.

What is the area of this sign?

A 36 in.²

C 160 in.²

B 72 in.²

D 320 in.²

2 The circular gym mat has a radius of 3 feet. What is the area of the gym mat?

A 3π ft²

C 9π ft²

B 6π ft²

D 36π ft²

3 A crystal is made of two triangular prisms.

The height of this crystal is 12 units. What is its volume?

A 960 cu units

C 1,440 cu units

B 1,280 cu units

D 1,920 cu units

4 The radius of a circular disc is 0.25 meter. What is the approximate circumference?

A 0.0625 m

C 0.785 m

B 0.19625 m

D 1.57 m

5 Each small cube in the diagram below has a side length of 10 millimeters.

What is the total surface area of the stack?

A 120 mm²

C 1,200 mm²

B 320 mm²

D 3,200 mm²

6 The diagram below shows the outline of a community swimming pool.

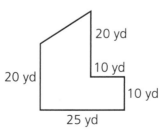

What is the total area of pool?

A 450 yd²

C 600 yd²

B 475 yd²

D 725 yd²

7 Kendra stores her craft tools in a plastic box that is the shape of a rectangular prism. The box is 8 inches long, 4 inches wide, and 3 inches tall. What is the surface area of the plastic box?

Answer _____

8 Felix folded two corners of a square piece of art paper as shown in the diagram here.

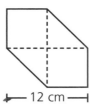

What is the area, in square centimeters, of the folded piece of paper?

— 12 cm —

Answer _____

9 A shipping container is in the shape of a rectangular prism. The container is 12 meters long, 3 meters wide, and 2.5 meters tall. What is the total volume, in cubic meters, of this prism?

Answer _____

10 A circle has a diameter of 8 inches. What is the approximate area, in square inches, of the circle? Use 3.14 for π.

Answer _____

11 The solid figure shown here is made up of a triangular prism and a rectangular prism.

What is the total surface area, in square feet, of the solid figure?

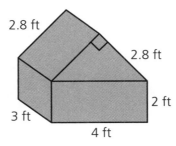

2.8 ft

2.8 ft

2 ft

3 ft

4 ft

Answer _____

12 A circular table has a diameter of 40 inches.

  Part A What is the circumference, in inches, of this table? Write your answer using π.

  Answer _____

  Part B What is the area, in square inches, of the table? Write your answer using π. Explain how you know.

  _____

  _____

  _____

13 This diagram shows a set of porch steps. Each step has the same width, depth, and height.

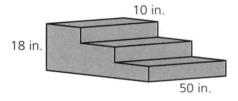

10 in.

18 in.

50 in.

  Part A What is the height, in inches, from one step to the next?

  Answer _____

  Part B What is the total volume, in cubic inches, of the steps? Show your work.

  Answer _____

Data, Statistics, and Probability

- **Lesson 1 Sampling** reviews what a sample is and how to find a random sample as well as how to draw conclusions from samples of data.

- **Lesson 2 Comparing Data Distributions** reviews how to compare two data sets visually and by using measures of center and variability.

- **Lesson 3 Probability** reviews what probability is and how to compute the probability of events that are equally likely to occur.

- **Lesson 4 Experimental Probability** reviews the difference between theoretical and experimental probabilities and how to use the results of experimental probability to make predictions.

- **Lesson 5 Compound Probability** reviews what a compound event is, how to find the sample space and probability of a compound event, and how to use simulations to approximate probabilities.

Sampling

7.SP.1, 7.SP.2

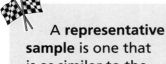

A **representative sample** is one that is as similar to the population being studied as possible.

Random samples are a good way to make sure a sample is representative.

The larger the sample, the more reliable the results.

Any inference on a population must be based on a smaller representative sample.

Gathering data on several random samples of the same size is a good way to make reliable inferences about a population.

Researchers sometimes collect data to study a **population,** or entire group of people or objects. Since it is difficult to collect data from an entire population, a sample of the population is often used. A **random sample** is a small set that is representative of the larger population.

A school principal wants to know how many hours a week each of the 624 students in the school spend reading for pleasure. She plans to survey a sample of students. What is an appropriate random sample she can use to collect her data?

The population is 624 students. The sample should be smaller than the total population but still representative of the entire set of students. The principal can survey about $\frac{1}{10}$, or 60, of these students. An appropriate sample would be to survey a few randomly chosen students from each homeroom class.

You can use proportions to make **inferences,** or predictions, about a population based on sample data.

In a survey of 150 town residents chosen at random, 90 of them are in favor of putting a new recreation center in town. The town has a total of 18,500 residents. About how many of the total residents are expected to be in favor of the new recreation center?

Set up a proportion to find *n,* the number of total residents in favor of the recreation center.

$$\frac{\text{residents in favor}}{\text{total residents}} \rightarrow \frac{90}{150} = \frac{n}{18{,}500}$$

Cross multiply to solve the proportion:

$$150n = 90(18{,}500)$$
$$150n = 1{,}665{,}000$$
$$n = 11{,}100$$

About 11,100 total residents are expected to be in favor of a new recreation center.

SAMPLE To help estimate the goose population in a certain area, scientists mark a total of 125 geese with tags. A few weeks later, they count 144 geese. Of these, 24 are marked with tags. What is a reasonable estimate for the total goose population in this area?

    A 149   **B** 750   **C** 864   **D** 3,000

The correct answer is B. Set up and solve a proportion using the ratio $\frac{\text{tagged geese}}{\text{total geese}}$. Let p represent the total goose population being estimated: $\frac{125}{p} = \frac{24}{144}$, $24p = 18,000$, $p = 750$. A reasonable estimate is 750 geese.

1 Harvey wants to know how long a car typically parks in the metered parking spaces in the center of town. He chooses to record the times 20 random cars are parked there one day. What is the sample of the data collected by Harvey?

    A all cars in the world

    B 20 random cars parked every day

    C 20 random cars parked one day

    D the cars belonging to each resident in town

2 There is an 85% chance that a flight on a certain airline will arrive on time. Out of a total of 600 flights, how many are expected to arrive on time?

    A 510   **C** 525

    B 515   **D** 585

3 A restaurant owner wants to know how often the customers in her restaurant eat out. Which sample will likely give the most reliable results?

    A the first 50 customers that come into the restaurant on Monday

    B every 10th customer to come into the restaurant on a weekend

    C 50 male customers arriving at different times two days in a row

    D 10 customers arriving at different times each day during one week

4 Sophie surveyed 30 random students in her school. Of these, 18 said they enjoy watching baseball. A total of 1,050 students are in the school. How many of these are expected to enjoy baseball?

    A 315   **C** 630

    B 504   **D** 735

SAMPLE A bag contains 400 colored chips. Without looking inside the bag, LaToya pulls out a handful of chips. She then notes the color of each chip, as shown in the list below.

blue	blue	yellow	red	red	red	blue	blue
yellow	red	green	green	red	blue	yellow	blue
blue	red	blue	blue	green	yellow	yellow	red

How many of the 400 total chips are expected to be blue?

Answer _____

> The colors of a total of 24 chips are listed in the sample. Of these, 9 are blue. So $\frac{9}{24}$ or $\frac{3}{8}$ of the sample are blue. This is a random sample since the chips were pulled from the bag without looking. So, of the total chips, $400 \times \frac{3}{8} = 150$ are expected to be blue.

5 Sean surveyed 208 American travelers at an airport. About 60% of those surveyed have been to a foreign country. Sean concludes that about 60% of all people in America have been to a foreign country. Is Sean's conclusion reasonable? Explain how you know.

_____

_____

_____

6 A quality control inspector looked at four samples of 30 picture frames each.

- He found 1 damaged frame in the first sample, 2 damaged frames in each of the next two samples, and 3 damaged frames in the fourth sample.

- The entire shipment has 450 frames.

What is a reasonable estimate for the total number of damaged picture frames to be expected in the entire shipment?

Answer _____

7 Tamika wants to know whether the students in her school prefer to use the library or the Internet to do research. She surveys all the students at her lunch table.

Part A Is the sample Tamika chose representative of the population she is interested in? Explain how you know.

Is this sample truly representative of the entire school population?

_____

_____

_____

_____

Part B Describe a different sample Tamika could use that would be representative of the population she is interested in.

_____

_____

_____

_____

8 A shipment of 12 boxes of 50 magazines each arrives at a newsstand. Rajiv opens up each box and looks at the top 5 magazines for damaged covers.

Part A Will this give him a reliable way to predict the total number of damaged magazines in the entire shipment? Why or why not?

_____

_____

_____

_____

Part B Suppose the chance of a cover being damaged is 3%. How many magazines in the shipment could Rajiv expect to have damaged covers?

Answer _____

Comparing Data Distributions

7.SP.3, 7.SP.4

The **mean** is the sum of all data points divided by the number of data points.

The **median** is the middle value in a set of ordered data points.

The **mode** is the value that occurs most frequently in a data set.

Range is the difference between the highest and lowest values in a data set.

Mean absolute deviation is the number that shows the average difference between the mean and each value in a data set.

• A small number indicates little variability since the values in the data set are close to the mean.

• A large number indicates greater variability since the values are farther from the mean.

The overall shape of data on a display can be symmetric or **skewed**, that is, unsymmetrical.

The **measure of center** in a data set is the number that summarizes all data points. Measures of center include the mean, median, and mode. The **measure of variability** is the number that describes how the points in a data set vary. Measures of variability include the range and mean absolute deviation.

Compare the center and the variability of the data sets below.

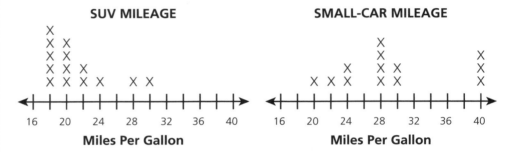

The SUV data is skewed to the left since most values are small numbers. The small-car data is more symmetric. So, the measure of center is greater for small cars than for SUVs.

The SUV data points are closer together than the data points for small cars. So, the measure of variability is also greater for small cars than for SUVs.

Measures of center and variability can also be found without a data display to compare two sets of data.

Look at the data in sets A and B.

Set A: {96, 75, 80, 88, 90, 93, 79, 70, 82}
Set B: {86, 87, 92, 94, 90, 92, 92, 89, 87}

Which data set has a smaller median?

When ordered from least to greatest, the values in set A range from 70 to 96 with a median, or middle value, of 82. The values in set B range from 86 to 94 with a median of 90. So set A has the smaller median.

SAMPLE The data sets below show the age of each player participating on two different sports teams.

Team 1: {23, 24, 24, 25, 26, 26, 27}

Team 2: {19, 21, 22, 23, 24, 24, 28}

Which statement is true of the mean absolute deviation of the data sets?

A   It is about twice as great for team 1 as for team 2.

B   It is about twice as great for team 2 as for team 1.

C   It is about four times as great for team 1 as for team 2.

D   It is about four times as great for team 2 as for team 1.

The correct answer is B. The mean age for team 1 is 25. The mean absolute deviation for team 1 is $\frac{2 + 1 + 1 + 0 + 1 + 1 + 2}{7} = 1\frac{1}{7}$. The mean age for team 2 is 23. The mean absolute deviation for team 2 is $\frac{4 + 2 + 1 + 0 + 1 + 1 + 5}{7} = 2$. So, the mean absolute deviation for team 2 is about twice that of team 1.

---

1 The data below shows the number of seats in each theater of two movie complexes.

Movie Complex P: {95, 125, 160, 212}

Movie Complex Q: {115, 125, 135, 155}

Which statement is true?

A   The mode for complex P is smaller than the mode for complex Q.

B   The mode for complex Q is smaller than the mode for complex P.

C   The median for complex P is smaller than the median for complex Q.

D   The median for complex Q is smaller than the median for complex P.

2 Which stem-and-leaf plot has a lower mean absolute deviation than store X?

DVD PRICES AT STORE X

0	9
1	4
2	2 7
3	0

1|5 means $15

A   **STORE A**

0	5
1	0 5 5
2	0
3	0

1|5 means $15

C   **STORE C**

0	
1	5 8
2	0 0 1
3	

1|5 means $15

B   **STORE B**

0	7 9
1	2
2	0
3	3

1|5 means $15

D   **STORE D**

0	
1	3 7 9
2	
3	5 5

1|5 means $15

SAMPLE The line plots below show the times, in minutes, for each route on two different bus lines.

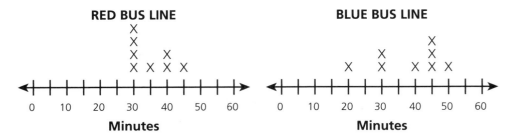

A bus from both the red bus line and the blue bus line leave at 2:00 P.M. Which bus line is more likely to end its route sooner?

Answer _____

The mode is a good indicator of the typical length of each bus line's routes. The mode for the red bus line is 30 minutes. The mode for the blue bus line is 45 minutes. Since a route on the red bus line is typically shorter than a route on the blue bus line, the red bus line is likely to end its route sooner.

3 Look at the data in the table below.

Set X	22.25	16.5	18.05	13	28	20.45
Set Y	9	14	40	6	5	21

Which data set has a smaller mean? Which has a smaller range?

Smaller mean _____   **Smaller range** _____

4 The table shows the number of text messages Alexa and Leann sent to each other during the past four weeks.

Week	1	2	3	4
Alexa	21	33	16	10
Leann	18	24	22	18

Alexa thinks since the mean number of text messages is the same for both her and Leann, the mean absolute deviations must also be the same. Is her thinking correct? Explain how you know.

_____

_____

5 This line plot shows the price, in dollars, per pound of each type of apple sold at Save-More Supermarket.

SAVE-MORE APPLE PRICES

Price Per Pound ($)

Part A Describe the measures of center and variability for this data set. Use the median and the range.

_____

_____

_____

Part B The median is greater for the price per pound of the same apples at Shopper's Haven. However, the range is smaller. In the space below, draw a line plot that shows the possible prices, in dollars, per pound of each type of apple sold at Shopper's Haven.

Would the data points need to be closer together or farther apart to show a smaller variability?

Probability

7.SP.5, 7.SP.7.a

An **event** is a situation or experiment that can have many different results, or **outcomes.**

If an event is certain, its probability is 1.

If an event is somewhat likely, its probability is around $\frac{1}{2}$.

If an event is impossible, its probability is 0.

An event chosen at random means that every item in the event has an equal chance of being chosen.

Probability can be expressed as a fraction, a decimal, or a percent.
$\frac{1}{10} = 0.1 = 10\%$

Probability is the measure of how likely an event is to occur. It is expressed as a number between 0 and 1. Probabilities can be impossible, unlikely, somewhat likely, highly likely, or certain.

> A fish tank has 40 orange fish, 4 blue fish, and 6 black fish. A fish is chosen from the tank at random. Describe the likelihood that the chosen fish will be a) orange or b) yellow.

Most of the fish are orange. Only a few are either blue or black. So, it is highly likely that an orange fish will be chosen.

None of the fish are yellow. So, it is impossible that one can be chosen.

To find the probability, P, of an event where each outcome is equally likely, use this formula:

$$P = \frac{\text{number of favorable outcomes}}{\text{number of possible outcomes}}$$

This chart describes the fish in a tank.

	Solid Color	Striped
Orange	35	5
Blue	4	0
Black	2	4

What is the probability that a fish chosen at random from the tank will be a striped orange fish?

The number of favorable outcomes is the number of striped orange fish: 5

The number of possible outcomes is the total number of fish in the tank: 35 + 5 + 4 + 2 + 4 = 50

Write the number of favorable outcomes over the number of possible outcomes: $P = \frac{5}{50} = \frac{1}{10}$

The probability of choosing a striped orange fish is $\frac{1}{10}$.

SAMPLE This spinner is divided into 8 equal sections.

Chen spins the arrow on this spinner once. What is the probability that the arrow will land on a vowel?

A $\frac{1}{8}$ B $\frac{1}{6}$ C $\frac{1}{4}$ D $\frac{1}{2}$

The correct answer is C. Use the formula for probability: $P = \dfrac{\text{number of favorable outcomes}}{\text{number of possible outcomes}}$. There are 2 vowels, A and E. So there are 2 favorable outcomes. There are 8 letters on the spinner. So there are 8 possible outcomes. The probability of landing on a vowel is $\frac{2}{8} = \frac{1}{4}$.

1 The probability it will rain tomorrow is 20%. Which word or words best describes the likelihood of it raining tomorrow?

A certain   C impossible

B unlikely   D highly likely

2 A number cube has the numbers 1–6. What is the probability than the number 5 results after the number cube is rolled?

A $\frac{1}{6}$ C $\frac{1}{2}$

B $\frac{1}{5}$ D $\frac{5}{1}$

3 It is neither likely nor unlikely that Cora will sit in the front of the bus tomorrow. Which probability best describes this event?

A 0   C 1

B 0.5   D 2.5

4 This list shows the number of cans of beans Taariq bought.

- 3 black beans
- 1 pinto bean
- 2 garbanzo beans
- 4 kidney beans

Taariq chooses one of these cans at random for a soup recipe. Which type of bean has a $\frac{1}{5}$ chance of being chosen?

A black   C garbanzo

B pinto   D kidney

5 Ji Sun scored 12 points out of her last 20 tries. What is the probability Ji Sun will score a point on her next try?

A 0.12   C 0.4

B 0.32   D 0.6

SAMPLE Emily rolls a 1–6 number cube. What is the probability that a number greater than 2 results after the cube is rolled?

Answer _____

> A 1–6 number cube has 6 possible outcomes: 1, 2, 3, 4, 5, or 6. The favorable outcomes are numbers greater than 2. They are 3, 4, 5, and 6. There are 4 favorable outcomes. So, the probability of rolling a number greater than 2 is $\frac{4}{6} = \frac{2}{3}$.

6 Describe an event that is highly likely to occur.

_____

_____

7 A set of cards contains the letters shown below.

K	N	I	C	K	K	N	A	C	K	S

What is the probability that a letter chosen at random will be a K?

Answer _____

8 A cooler contains these bottles of flavored water: 4 blueberry, 5 peach, 1 raspberry, and 2 lemon. One bottle of water is chosen at random. What is the probability the bottle of water will be blueberry flavored?

Answer _____

9 There are 5 quarters, 12 dimes, and 24 pennies in a piggy bank. One of these coins is chosen at random. Describe an event that is certain to occur.

Answer _____

10 The owner of a music store surveyed some customers about their favorite type of music. The results of the survey are shown in this table.

MUSIC SURVEY

Type of Music	Number of People
Classical	8
Rock	36
Hip-hop	11
Country	20
Other	45

One of these customers will be selected at random to win a gift card to the music store.

Part A Is it unlikely, somewhat likely, or highly likely that the selected customer answered "hip-hop" in the survey? Explain how you know.

_____

_____

Part B What is the probability the selected customer chose "rock" as the favorite type of music? Explain how you know.

How do you find the total possible outcomes from this survey?

_____

_____

_____

_____

Experimental Probability

7.SP.6, 7.SP.7.b

The formula for theoretical probability is

$$P = \frac{\text{favorable outcomes}}{\text{possible outcomes}}$$

A **trial** is an event from experimental data or observations.

When used to make predictions, experimental probability gives a reasonable estimate, **not** an exact amount.

Theoretical probability is the measure of how likely an event is to occur when each outcome is equally likely. **Experimental probability** is based on repeated trials from an experiment or observations. Outcomes in experimental probability are **not** equally likely.

To find the experimental probability, P, of an event, use this formula:

$$P = \frac{\text{number of times event occurs}}{\text{total number of trials}}$$

A fair coin is flipped once. It can land either heads-side up or tails-side up. The theoretical probability of the coin landing heads-side up is $\frac{1}{2}$.

A fair coin is flipped 100 times. The coin lands heads-side up 45 of those times. The experimental probability of landing heads-side up is $\frac{45}{100}$ or $\frac{9}{20}$.

You can make predictions for the likelihood of future events based on the results of experimental data.

A sample of 200 tires is inspected for defects. Of those, 8 tires have defects. Based on these results, what is the expected number of tires with defects in a set of 2,500 tires?

Find the experimental probability of a tire having defects.

$$P = \frac{8}{200} \text{ or } \frac{1}{25}$$

Multiply this probability by the total number of tires in the set.

$$2{,}500 \cdot \frac{1}{25} = 100$$

About 100 tires from the set of 2,500 are expected to have defects.

UNIT 7
Data, Statistics, and Probability

SAMPLE The arrow on this spinner is spun 50 times.

The arrow lands on the heart a total of 10 times. What type of probability is used to show the chances of the arrow landing on the heart on the next spin?

A theoretical because the heart results $\frac{1}{4}$ of the time

B theoretical because the heart results $\frac{1}{5}$ of the time

C experimental because the heart results $\frac{1}{4}$ of the time

D experimental because the heart results $\frac{1}{5}$ of the time

The correct answer is D. The theoretical probability for each event would be $\frac{1}{4}$, since each outcome is equally likely. With experimental probability, each outcome is not always equally likely. The actual probability of the arrow landing on the heart is $\frac{10}{50} = \frac{1}{5}$, so experimental probability is used.

1 A 1–6 number cube is rolled 60 times. The number 3 results 15 times. What is the experimental probability of rolling a 3?

A $\frac{1}{6}$ C $\frac{1}{3}$

B $\frac{1}{4}$ D $\frac{1}{2}$

2 A spinner contains 3 equal-sized sections of red, yellow, and blue. The arrow on this spinner is spun 150 times. Which of the following best describes the experimental probability of the arrow landing on red for these trials?

A exactly 30 times

B close to 30 times

C exactly 50 times

D close to 50 times

3 Steve flipped a coin 40 times. The coin landed tails-side up 24 times. If Steve flipped the coin a total of 500 times, what would be the expected number of times it would land tails-side up?

A 60   C 300

B 240   D 350

4 Erin made 3 free throws and missed 2 free throws in her last basketball game. How many free throws would Erin be expected to make on her next 30 attempts based on her last game?

A 10   C 20

B 18   D 24

SAMPLE This table shows the number of brothers and sisters the students in Jerry's class have.

A total of 450 students are in Jerry's school. He predicts that about 90 of the students have no brothers or sisters based on these data. Is his prediction reasonable? Explain how you know.

NUMBER OF BROTHERS AND SISTERS	
Brothers and Sisters	Number of Students
0	8
1	4
2	9
3	3
4	1

Answer _____

According to the given data, there are 8 students who have 0 brothers or sisters. So the experimental probability of not having any brothers or sisters is $\frac{8}{8 + 4 + 9 + 3 + 1} = \frac{8}{25} = 0.32$. A reasonable prediction for the total students would be $0.32 \times 450 = 144$. Since 90 is not close to 144, it is not a reasonable estimate.

5 Levi made 50 phone calls during a charity fund-raising drive and received 4 pledges for donations. If he makes 120 calls, about how many pledges could Levi expect?

Answer _____

6 Padma spun the arrow on this spinner 250 times.

The arrow landed on a square 60 times. How do the theoretical and experimental probabilities of the arrow landing on a square compare?

_____

_____

_____

_____

7 Zoe tosses a cone-shaped party hat into the air. She reasons that the hat will land upright or it won't, so the probability of the hat landing upright must be $\frac{1}{2}$.

Part A Is Zoe's reasoning correct? Explain how you know.

_____

_____

_____

_____

> What conditions must be present for the hat to have an equally likely chance of landing upright?

Part B Zoe then tosses a postcard in the air 25 times. Of those times, the picture side lands face up 10 times. If Zoe tosses the postcard in the air a total of 80 times, about how many times is the picture side expected to land face up? Explain how you know.

_____

_____

_____

8 Willa rolls a 1–6 number cube once.

Part A What is the probability Willa rolls a number less than 4?

　　　　Answer _____

Part B Willa then rolls the number cube a total of 25 times. The number 2 results 5 times. What type of probability, theoretical or experimental, would be used to show the chances of the number 2 resulting on the next roll? Explain how you know.

_____

_____

_____

Compound Probability

7.SP.8.a–c

A **tree diagram** is a visual representation of outcomes using branches.

First flip Second flip Outcome

H ⟨ H —— H, H
    T —— H, T

T ⟨ H —— T, H
    T —— T, T

A **sample space** is a list of all possible outcomes in an experiment.

You can also find the probability of compound events by multiplying the probability of each separate event.

Different simulations testing the same experiment can have different results. The more trials run in a simulation, the more accurate the result will be.

Remember that 0 is an even number.

A **compound event** consists of two or more events. The probability of a compound event can be found using lists, tables, or tree diagrams.

Aimee will flip a fair coin 3 times. What is the probability that the coin will land heads-side up exactly once?

Make a list of the sample space for the 3 coin flips.

H = heads, T = tails

HHH	HHT	HTH	HTT
TTT	TTH	THT	THH

There are a total of 8 possible outcomes. Heads results exactly once in 3 of the possible outcomes.

So, the probability that heads results exactly once in 3 coin flips is $P = \frac{3}{8}$.

You can also use a **simulation,** or experiment, to find the probability of compound events. One kind of simulation uses random digits generated by a calculator or online program.

Cole wants to know the experimental probability that 2 coins will have the same result when flipped. Explain how he could use a simulation to find this.

Use random digits to represent heads and tails. Let each even digit represent heads and each odd digit represent tails. Run several trials. Below are the random digits generated by 30 trials.

04	39	91	98	75	33	93	62	52	50
99	54	66	34	11	20	03	40	26	18
79	80	70	10	09	95	18	98	33	26

Count the pairs that have both even digits and both odd digits. There are 14 pairs. So, the experimental probability that 2 flipped coins will have the same result is $\frac{18}{30}$ or $\frac{3}{5}$.

SAMPLE Gabby wants to know the probability that in a family of 3 children, the 2 oldest children are girls. For each trial, she flips a coin 3 times to conduct the simulation shown below.

HHH   HTH   TTH   HTT   HHT   THH   HTT   THT   HHT   TTT
HHH   THH   HHT   HTT   HTH   THH   TTT   THH   HHT   THT

H represents a girl, and T represents a boy. Based on this simulation, what is the probability that the 2 oldest children are girls?

A $\frac{1}{4}$ B $\frac{3}{10}$ C $\frac{1}{3}$ D $\frac{1}{2}$

The correct answer is B. Count the number of outcomes that have H as the first two results. There are a total of 6 outcomes with either HHH or HHT. The total number of outcomes is 20. So, the probability is $\frac{6}{20} = \frac{3}{10}$.

1 A 1–6 number cube is rolled twice. How many possible outcomes are in the sample space?

A   2   C   12

B   6   D   36

Use these spinners to answer questions 2 and 3.

2 Alex spins the arrows on the two spinners and adds the results. What is the sample space of all possible outcomes?

A {1, 2}   C {2, 3, 4, 5}

B {1, 2, 3}   D {1, 2, 3, 4, 5}

3 What is the probability that a sum of 4 will result when both arrows are spun once?

A $\frac{1}{2}$ C $\frac{1}{4}$

B $\frac{1}{3}$ D $\frac{1}{5}$

4 Two-thirds of the gumballs in a jar are red. How can a 1–6 number cube be used to find the probability that a gumball chosen at random from the jar will be red?

A   Let the number 1 represent a red gumball.

B   Let the numbers 2 and 3 represent a red gumball.

C   Let the numbers 1, 2, and 3 represent a red gumball.

D   Let the numbers 1, 2, 3 and 4 represent a red gumball.

SAMPLE Kelli spins the arrow on this spinner two times. What is the probability that an odd number results both times?

Answer _____

First find the sample space showing all possible outcomes. Show the possible outcomes of the two spins in parentheses: (first spin, second spin).

(1, 1) (1, 2) (1, 3)

(2, 1) (2, 2) (2, 3)

(3, 1) (3, 2) (3, 3)

There are 9 total outcomes. Of these, 4 have odd numbers for both spins. So, the probability is $\frac{4}{9}$.

5 Bernardo flips a coin and rolls a 1–6 number cube. In the space below, draw a tree diagram to show the set of all possible outcomes.

6 Lillian flips a fair coin three times. What is the probability that at least one of the flips results in the coin facing tails-side up?

Answer _____

7 A train is early $\frac{1}{6}$ of the time, on time $\frac{1}{2}$ of the time, and late $\frac{1}{3}$ of the time. Doreen wants to know the probability that the train will be late two times in a row.

Part A Explain how two 1–6 number cubes can be used to simulate this situation.

_____

_____

_____

_____

_____

_____

What numbers on the number cube could represent the train being late?

Part B Use two 1–6 number cubes to perform a simulation to find the probability that the train is late two times in a row. Show your work.

Write the probability you found in your simulation as a percent.

Answer _____

REVIEW

Data, Statistics, and Probability

Read each problem. Circle the letter of the best answer.

1 It is not very likely that it will rain tomorrow. Which probability best describes this event?

   A 0   **C** 0.5

   B 0.1   **D** 1

2 From a random sample of 40 people at a banquet, 15 ordered the chicken dinner. If there are a total of 212 people at the banquet, about how many chicken dinners are ordered?

   A 40   **C** 80

   B 60   **D** 100

3 One card from set X is multiplied by one card from set Y.

Set X: [1] [2] [3] Set Y: [4] [5] [6]

What is the sample space of all possible outcomes?

   A {4, 5, 6}

   B {5, 6, 7, 8, 9}

   C {1, 2, 3, 4, 5, 6}

   D {4, 5, 6, 8, 10, 12, 15, 18}

4 Miranda rolls a 1–6 number cube 60 times. Which best describes the experimental probability of the cube landing on 6 during these trials?

   A exactly 6 times   **C** exactly 10 times

   B close to 6 times   **D** close to 10 times

5 The line plots below show the ratings two different groups of people gave a new movie.

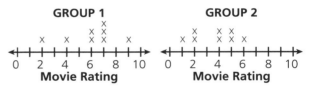

Which statement best describes these plots?

   A The center and variability for group 1 are greater than for group 2.

   B The center and variability for group 2 are greater than for group 1.

   C The center for group 1 is greater and the variability for group 2 is greater.

   D The center for group 2 is greater and the variability for group 1 is greater.

6 Andre flips a fair coin 4 times. What is the probability that exactly 2 flips will result in heads and 2 flips will result in tails?

Answer _____

7 A spinner is divided into 12 equal sections and numbered 1–12. Emmanuel spins the arrow on the spinner. What is the probability that the arrows lands on a number less than 5?

Answer _____

8 Sanjay recorded the number of days it was sunny last month. In the past 30 days, it was sunny 80% of the time. Sanjay concludes that it will be sunny 80% of the year. Is his conclusion reasonable? Explain.

_____

_____

9 Lydia rolled a 1–6 number cube 120 times and recorded the results in the table here. Is the theoretical probability of rolling a number divisible by 3 greater than, less than, or the same as the experimental probability? Explain.

Number	1	2	3	4	5	6
Number of Rolls	20	16	24	21	27	12

_____

_____

_____

10 Each spinner below is divided into equal-sized sections.

Paul will spin the arrow on each spinner once. What is the probability that an even number results both times?

Answer _____

11 Look at the team data in the table below.

Team A	72	73	69	70	71	74
Team B	75	70	69	67	70	68

Part A Which team has a greater measure of center? Which team has a greater measure of variability?

Center _____   **Variability** _____

Part B Explain how you know.

_____

_____

_____

_____

12 There is a 50% chance that it will snow each of the next 3 days. Fay wants to know the probability that it will snow all three days.

Part A Explain how a fair coin can be used to simulate this situation.

_____

_____

_____

_____

Part B Perform a simulation to find the probability that it will snow all three days. Show your work.

Write the probability you found in your simulation as a percent.

Answer _____

PRACTICE TEST

Read each problem. Circle the letter of the best answer.

1 Which pair of x and y quantities is **not** proportional to the others?

x	y
6	9
8	12
16	20
18	27

A   6 and 9

B   8 and 12

C   16 and 20

D   18 and 27

2 Bianca climbed 1,250 feet up a mountain. Then she climbed 1,250 feet down the mountain. What was her change in height?

A   0 feet

B   1,250 feet

C   2,250 feet

D   2,500 feet

3 Which shape represents the horizontal cross section of this prism?

A

B

C

D

4 Brent earned $90 for working 12 hours. How much would he earn for working 20 hours?

A $110

B $120

C $150

D $180

5 Audrey spins the arrow on this spinner.

What is the probability that the arrow lands on a number greater than 2?

A $\frac{1}{9}$

C $\frac{2}{3}$

B $\frac{1}{3}$

D $\frac{7}{9}$

6 Yolanda bought a jacket on sale for 25% off the regular price. Which expression can be used to find the amount she paid for the jacket with a regular price of p dollars?

A   0.25p

C   1.25p

B   0.75p

D   2.25p

7 Which number line models the expression $4 - (-1)$?

A

B

C

D

8 The unit rate for a proportional relationship is 9 cents per ounce. Which point must be located on the graph of this proportional relationship?

A (0, 9)   **C** (9, 0)

B (1, 9)   **D** (9, 1)

9 Scott tossed a wad of paper. It landed in the trash can 3 times and missed 2 times. Based on these results, how many times would Scott expect the wad of paper to land in the trash can if he throws it 60 times?

A 20   **C** 40

B 36   **D** 48

10 Which expression has the same value as $-24 - (-17)$?

A $17 - 24$ **C** $24 - 17$

B $-17 + 24$ **D** $24 + 17$

11 From a random sample of 36 students, 16 are planning to go to the school's first football game. There is a total of 248 students. About how many are planning to go to the football game?

A 110   **C** 140

B 125   **D** 175

12 The cost of a wood board is proportional to its length. A 5-foot board costs $3.50. Which equation can be used to find the cost, y, of a board x feet long?

A $y = 0.175x$ **C** $y = 1.5x$

B $y = 0.7x$ **D** $y = 17.5x$

13 What is the fully factored form of the expression shown below?

$$18n^3 + 48n^2 - 36n - 24$$

A $6(3n^3 + 8n^2 - 6n - 4)$

B $3(6n^3 + 16n^2 - 12n - 8)$

C $3(6n^3 + 48n^2 - 36n - 24)$

D $6(3n^3 + 48n^2 - 36n - 24)$

14 Angles Y and Z are supplementary. The measure of $\angle Y$ is 69°. Which equation can be used to find $m\angle Z$?

A $69° + m\angle Z = 90°$

B $69° - m\angle Z = 90°$

C $69° + m\angle Z = 180°$

D $69° - m\angle Z = 180°$

15 A new car costs $22,645. The tax rate on the car is 6%. What is the best estimate for the total cost of the car including tax?

A $23,000   C $25,000

B $24,000   D $26,000

16 Keira will roll a 1–6 number cube and spin the arrow on this spinner.

How many items are in the sample space of outcomes?

A 2   C 22

B 11   D 30

17 What is the value of $-4\frac{1}{3} \times 1\frac{1}{2}$?

A 4.167   C 6.5

B -4.167…   D -6.5

18 What value of x makes this equation true?

$$-0.2x - 1.8 = 3$$

A -24   C 6

B -6   D 24

19 What is the factored form of $60n + 108$?

A $6(10n + 12)$ C $12(5n + 9)$

B $6(10n + 108)$ D $12(5n + 108)$

20 The stem-and-leaf plots below show the average monthly rainfall in two cities.

CITY 1		CITY 2	
0	8	0	
1	1 5 7 8	1	
2	3	2	
3	2 5	3	1
4	0	4	4 5 6 9
5	4 8 9	5	1 5 8 8
6		6	0 1 1

1|7 means 1.7 in.   4|5 means 4.5 in.

Which statement best compares these plots?

A The median for city 1 is the same as for city 2.

B The median for city 1 is greater than for city 2.

C The range for city 1 is the same as for city 2.

D The range for city 1 is greater than for city 2.

21 The temperature at 9:00 was -4.2° C. An hour later, it was -2.6° C. Which expression represents the change in temperature during the hour?

A -2.6 + 4.2   C -4.2 + 2.6

B -2.6 - 4.2   D -4.2 - 2.6

22 Which expression has the same value as -0.6 × 93?

A $-0.6 \cdot 100 - 7$

B $-0.6 - 100 \cdot 7$

C $-0.6 \cdot (100 - 7)$

D $-0.6 \cdot (100 \cdot 7)$

23 The perimeter of the triangle below is $6p + 2q - 5$ units.

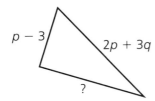

Which expression represents the length, in units, of the missing side of this triangle?

A $3p - q - 2$ **C** $3p + 3q - 2$

B $3p + q - 8$ **D** $3p + 5q - 8$

24 A circular cookie cutter has a radius of 4 centimeters. What is the area of the cookie cutter?

A 4π in.^{2} **C** 16π in.^{2}

B 8π in.^{2} **D** 64π in.^{2}

25 The probability a train car will be full is 60%. Which word or words best describes the likelihood the train car will be full?

A certain   **C** highly likely

B unlikely   **D** somewhat likely

26 A rental car company charges $18 per day and $0.25 per mile driven to rent a car. Which expression shows the total daily cost to rent a car driven m miles?

A $18m + 0.25$ **C** $18(m + 0.25)$

B $0.25m + 18$ **D** $0.25(m + 18)$

27 Each small cube in the diagram below has a side length of 1 centimeter.

What is the total surface area of the stack of cubes?

A 11 cm^2 **C** 30 cm^2

B 22 cm^2 **D** 36 cm^2

28 Seth took at most 45 minutes to do his reading homework. He read each page in 2 minutes and wrote a summary in 5 minutes. Which inequality can be used to find p, the number of pages Seth read?

A $2p + 15 \geq 45$

B $2 + p + 15 \geq 45$

C $2p + 15 \leq 45$

D $2 + p + 15 \leq 45$

29 Which is the solution to the inequality $-5x + 20 > 15$?

A $x > 1$

B $x < 1$

C $x > -7$

D $x < -7$

30 The diagram below represents the shape of Eva's deck.

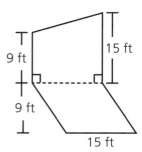

What is the total area of the deck?

A   315 ft²

B   475 ft²

C   495 ft²

D   540 ft²

31 Ty has a 50% chance of answering a trivia question correctly. He wants to know the probability that he will answer at least 3 of 4 trivia questions correctly. He flips a coin to conduct the simulation shown below.

HHTH   HHTT   THHT   HHHH   THTT
THHT   THHT   HTTH   THTT   HHHH
THTT   THTT   HTHT   HHTT   THTT
TTHT   HHTH   THHT   HHTT   THTH

H represents a correct answer, and T represents an incorrect answer. Based on this simulation, what is the probability that he answers at least 3 trivia questions correctly?

A $\frac{1}{4}$

B $\frac{1}{5}$

C $\frac{2}{5}$

D $\frac{3}{4}$

32 A radio station plays $3\frac{1}{2}$ minutes of commercials every $\frac{1}{4}$ hour. At this rate, how many minutes of commercials does this radio station play in 1 hour?

Answer _____

33 This table shows a proportional relationship.

Number of People	6	8	9	15
Total Admission ($)	72	96	108	180

Write the ratio that is common throughout this table, in simplest form.

Answer _____

34 In the diagram below, m∠1 = 58°.

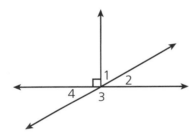

What is m∠3?

Answer _____

35 Write this expression in simplest form.

$$(5a + b) - 2(3a + 4b)$$

Answer _____

36 Cedric will roll a 1–6 number cube twice. What is the probability that a number greater than 4 results both times?

Answer _____

37 The value of the expression (-6 ÷ n) is **not** a rational number. What must be the value of n?

Answer _____

38 A storage crate is in the shape of a rectangular prism. The crate is 2 feet long, $1\frac{1}{2}$ feet wide, and $1\frac{1}{2}$ feet tall. What is the total volume, in cubic feet, of this crate?

Answer _____

39 What is the approximate circumference, in square centimeters, of the circle shown here? Use 3.14 for π.

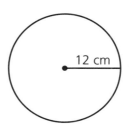

12 cm

Answer _____

40 What is the value of the expression below?

$$-8.5 + 3(2.5)$$

Answer _____

41 Look at the data in the table below.

Set A	38	35	24	61	40	43
Set B	25	39	51	47	42	48

Which data set has a smaller measure of center, set A or set B? Explain how you know.

_____

_____

_____

42 The clearance price of a book is $9. The original price of the book was $25. By what percent was the price of this book decreased?

Answer _____

43 What value of *w* makes this equation true?

$$-5w + 1 = 9$$

Answer _____

44 Ethan cut a block of wood in the shape shown here.

What is the total surface area, in square centimeters, of the shape?

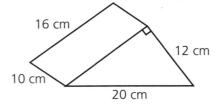

Answer _____

45 Does the equation $5 \times 0 = 0$ show the multiplicative identity property? Explain how you know.

_____

_____

46 Vera counts the first 10 cars to enter the teachers' parking lot at school one morning. Of those, 40% of the cars were red. She concludes that 40% of all the cars in the teachers' parking lot will be red. Given her sample, is Vera's conclusion reasonable? Explain how you know.

_____

_____

47 What is the area, in square feet, of the polygon below?

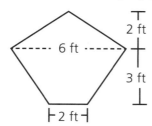

Answer _____

48 Tess factors the expression $36h^3 + 48h^2 - 60h - 24$ as shown below.

$$4(9h^3 + 12h^2 - 15h - 6)$$

Is this expression fully factored? How can you tell?

_____

_____

49 In the space below, draw and label a triangle with two sides measuring 3 centimeters and 6 centimeters and the angle between them measuring 80°.

50 Marcus tosses a coin into the air 64 times. It lands tails-side up 30 times. From this data, can the theoretical or experimental probability be found? Explain how you know.

_____

_____

_____

_____

Read the problem. Write your answer.

51 Part of a lunch menu is shown below.

Lunch Menu

Pizza	small	$ 9.50
	large	$13.50
Salad		$ 3.50
Juice		$ 1.25

Part A Deborah and two friends share the cost of a large pizza. Deborah also buys a salad and a juice. Write an expression to show the total amount, in dollars, Deborah pays. Then find the amount.

Answer ____________________________

Part B There is a 5% tax on all lunch orders. What is the total cost, including tax, for one small pizza, two salads, and two juices? Show your work.

Answer __________

52 Shiro spins the arrows on these two spinners once.

Part A In the space below, draw a tree diagram or make a list to show the set of all possible outcomes.

Part B What is the probability that the arrows will land on two odd numbered sections? Explain how you found your answer.

_____

_____

_____

53 A scale drawing of Nadia's kitchen floor is shown below.

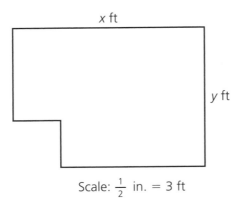

Scale: $\frac{1}{2}$ in. = 3 ft

Part A Use your inch ruler to find the actual lengths, in feet, for the sides labeled *x* and *y*.

Answer _____

Part B What is the area, in square feet, of the kitchen floor? Explain how you know.

_____

_____

_____

_____

GLOSSARY

absolute value   the distance of a number from 0 on a number line

additive identity   0; the number that when added to any other number equals the other number

additive inverse   the opposite of a number; the number that when added to another number results in a sum of 0

adjacent angles   angles that are next to each other, sharing a common ray

algebraic expression   an expression that contains symbols, or letters, and numbers and operations

area   the space inside a plane figure, measured in square units

area formulas   equations used to find the area of plane figures:

circle: $A = \pi r^2 = 3.14 \times$ radius squared

rectangle: $A = lw =$ length $\times$ width

parallelogram: $A = bh =$ base $\times$ height

triangle: $A = \frac{1}{2}bh = \frac{1}{2} \times$ base $\times$ height

trapezoid: $A = \frac{1}{2}(b_1 + b_2)h = \frac{1}{2} \times$ (base$_1$ + base$_2$) $\times$ height

associative property   allows numbers to be grouped with parentheses and then to be added or multiplied, with the same sum or product: $a + (b + c) = (a + b) + c$ and $a \times (b \times c) = (a \times b) \times c$

circumference   the distance around a circle. The formula for circumference is $C = \pi d = 3.14 \times$ diameter.

coefficient   a number that is in front of a variable

commutative property   allows numbers to be added or multiplied in any order, with the same sum or product: $a + b = b + a$ and $a \times b = b \times a$

compatible numbers   numbers that are easy to compute with

complementary angles	two angles whose measures sum to 90°
complex fraction	a fraction that has a fraction in the numerator, the denominator, or both
composite figure	a shape made up of more than one figure
compound event	an event consisting of two or more events
constant	a value that does not change, such as a unit rate
coordinate plane	two number lines placed at right angles that are used to locate points in space
cross product	the product of the denominator of one fraction and the numerator of the other
cross section	the resulting plane figure when a three-dimensional shape is sliced

diameter	the distance across the center of a circle
distributive property	allows a number to be multiplied by a sum or each addend to be multiplied separately and the products added, with the same result: $a(b + c) = ab + ac$

equation	a number sentence that shows two expressions are equal
equivalent expressions	expressions that represent the same value
estimate	to find an approximate value
event	a situation or experiment that can have different results, or outcomes
experimental probability	a measure based on repeated trials from an experiment or observations. Outcomes in experimental probability are *not* equally likely.
expression	a grouping of numbers, symbols, and operations that shows the value of something

factor	a number or expression that evenly divides into another with no remainder; to find the greatest number or expression that evenly divides each term of an algebraic expression

greatest common factor	the greatest number or expression that evenly divides into two or more numbers or expressions

identity property	allows 0 to be added to any number, with the result being the number, or allows 1 to multiply any number, with the result being the number: $a + 0 = a$ and $1 \times a = a$
inequality	a number sentence that compares two expressions using inequality symbols:

$<$ means "is less than"

$>$ means "is greater than"

$\leq$ means "is less than or equal to"

$\geq$ means "is greater than or equal to"

inferences	predictions
infinite	countless
integers	whole numbers, including 0, and their opposites
inverse operation	an operation that undoes another operation. Addition and subtraction are inverse operations. Multiplication and division are inverse operations.
inverse property	the sum of a number and its inverse equal 0: $a + (-a) = 0$; the product of a number and its inverse equal 1: $a \times \frac{1}{a} = 1$

like terms	terms that have the same variable parts

mean	the sum of the data values divided by the number of values; the average
mean absolute deviation	the number that shows the average difference between the mean and each value in a data set
measure of center	a number that summarizes all the numbers in the data set, such as mean, median, or mode
measure of variability	a number that describes how the numbers in a data set vary, such as range or mean absolute deviation
median	the number in the middle of a set of ordered data values
mode	the number that occurs most frequently in a data set

multiplicative identity	1; the number by which a second number is multiplied for a product of the second number: $a \times 1 = a$
multiplicative inverse	the reciprocal of a number; the number that multiplies another number for a product of 1
multi-step percent problems	problems involving more than one step, such as percent increase and decrease

opposites	numbers that are the same distance from 0 on a number line
origin	the center of a coordinate plane, located at the intersection of the x- and y-axes, having the coordinates (0, 0)
outcome	a possible result of an event

percent	a ratio that compares a number to 100, written with the symbol %
percent error	the percent that represents the difference between the measured and actual amounts
pi	a number with a value of 3.1415926…. An approximate value of pi is 3.14. The symbol for pi is π.
plane figure	a flat, two-dimensional shape such as a square, circle, or triangle
polygon	a plane geometric figure with straight sides
population	an entire group of people or objects
prism	a solid figure with two congruent polygon bases and rectangular sides
probability	the measure of how likely an event is to occur, expressed as a number between 0 and 1
proportion	an equation that shows that two ratios are equal
proportional relationship	a relationship between two quantities in which the value of x always changes by a unit rate to produce y, represented as an equation of the form $y = ax$
protractor	a tool used to measure the size of an angle

quadrilateral   a polygon with four sides

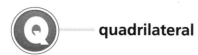 **radius**   the distance from the center of a circle to its edge

random sample   a small set that is representative of a larger population

range   the difference between the highest and lowest values in a data set

rate   a comparison between two quantities with different units of measure

rational number   any number that can be written as a fraction, including whole numbers, integers, fractions, and some decimals

reciprocal   the number by which another number is multiplied to equal a product of 1; the multiplicative inverse

repeating decimal   a decimal in which one or more digits repeat without end

representative sample   a sample that is as similar to the population being studied as possible

 **sample space**   a list of all possible outcomes in an experiment

scale   the ratio that compares the length of a scale drawing to the actual object

scale drawing   a diagram, model, or drawing that is larger or smaller than the actual object it represents

simulation   an experiment used to find the probability of a compound event

skewed   having unevenly distributed data values. Data skewed to the left has more data values at the low end; data skewed to the right has more data values at the high end.

solid figure   a three-dimensional figure that takes up space, such as a prism, pyramid, cylinder, or cone

solve   to find the value or values that make a number sentence true

supplementary angles   two angles whose measures sum to 180°

surface area	the sum of the areas of all the sides of a solid figure. The formula for the surface area of a rectangular prism is $SA = 2lw + 2lh + 2wh$.
symmetric	having evenly distributed data values

T

terminate	to stop
terminating decimal	a decimal that stops
terms	groups of numbers and variables
theoretical probability	the measure of how likely an event is to occur when each outcome is equally likely
tree diagram	a visual representation of outcomes using branches
trial	an event from experimental data or observations
triangle	a polygon with three sides

U

unit rate	a rate that compares a quantity to one unit

V

variable	a letter or symbol that represents an unknown value or a value that can change
vertical angles	opposite angles formed by intersecting lines, always congruent
volume	the amount of space inside a three-dimensional figure. The formula for volume of a rectangular prism is $V = l \times w \times h$.

Z

zero product property	any number multiplied by 0 has a product of 0: $a \times 0 = 0$